—— ⚬⚬⚬ ——

GOD BEHIND BARS

A Prison Chaplain Reflects on the Lord's Prayer

by
Pierre Raphael

PAULIST PRESS
New York/Mahwah, N.J.

All scripture quotations are taken from the Revised Standard Version.

This volume was translated from the French by Matthew O'Connell with further editing by Pat Ryan and Charles Mann.

Cover design by Cindy Dunne

Copyright © 1999. This book was originally published in French as *Notre Père qui es enfer* © 1977 by Desclee de Brouwer. The English translation © 1999 by Paulist Press, Inc.

Library of Congress Cataloging-in-Publication Data

Raphaël, Pierre.
    [Notre Père qui es en enfer. English]
    God behind bars : a prison chaplain reflects on the Lord's Prayer / by Pierre Raphaël.
      p.   cm.
    ISBN 0-8091-3868-9 (alk. paper)
    1. Lord's Prayer. 2. Church work with prisoners. I. Title.
BV230.R2613   1999
226.9´606–dc21   99–10067
                                         CIP

Published by Paulist Press
997 Macarthur Boulevard
Mahwah, New Jersey 07430

www.paulistpress.com

Printed and bound in the
United States of America

GOD BEHIND BARS

Contents

To my friends at Abraham House

My dear friends, the Lord's Prayer contains many great mysteries of our faith. In these few words there is great spiritual strength, for this summary of divine teaching contains all our prayers and petitions. And so, the Lord commands us:

"Pray then like this:
Our Father who art in heaven."

Treatise on the Lord's Prayer
Saint Cyprian, bishop and martyr, A.D. 200–58

"Maintain your soul in hell
and do not despair"

It is written that the Greek monk Staretz Silouan, who was canonized in 1988, heard the Lord say those words one day. In his monastery on Mount Athos, Silouan would live amid doubts, fears and great physical suffering until his death in 1938, but he received the grace of continual prayer. It is also said that he had the audacity to call God his Father and that he had deep compassion for every human being immersed in the daily drama of the world.

The Undistorted Image,
Archimandrite Sofrony

Introduction

I see people all around grappling with the question of how to pray. I see all of them praying as best they can, as best they know how. In my South Bronx neighborhood, I find an immense need for God. So many churches and chapels of every kind in so small an area. So much noise in the evening, when people shout the name of God. The preachers and believers are out there on the corner and a few feet away are drugs and human emptiness and all the violence anyone could imagine. Frenzied noise from loudspeakers, undigested words and the massive presence of a religious rumble on every side. Is this the Athens of Saint Paul and his Areopagus in our time?

All this noise can be as disconcerting as the sterile silence of the desert. Today there are so many deserts, and I have experienced some of them. For two years I marched as a draftee in the French army and lived in the rocks, sun and sand of the Sahara. In that place of seclusion and bitter extremes, it is very easy to feel totally powerless. Then in Appalachia, where I spent three years as a worker-priest (I was a welder), I found a desert of another sort, pockets of dire spiritual and material poverty. Now my desert is the South Bronx, where I work at Abraham House, a residential alternative to prison.

Before living in the South Bronx I was a chaplain at Rikers Island, New York City's penal colony, for sixteen years. During that time I witnessed the prison population increase from six to twenty thousand. The harshness of a jail, a place of brutal sterility like the desert, can force a person to confront long-buried questions and matters screened by everyday living.

This book grew out of my desire to confront the reality of the desert, whether in or out of prison, with prayer, especially the prayer of the Our Father. In the prisoners' bleak search for a way out of the pit, I have found that the Lord's Prayer is best able to overcome their brutalizing anger and despair. Even in such an unlikely place as prison, against all odds, this prayer has a potency far greater than other prayers. This power can be best expressed by the phrase that summarizes all the following pages: the Lord's Prayer puts an end to prison and turns the desert into fertile land.

Each of us is unique, but as we learn from the Our Father, our different experiences are related. When we choose to climb a mountain, we find that there are many ways to the summit. Because there is only one top, though, even if we start at different points, our paths are moving closer and closer together. Just as we find convergences in a journey such as this, so, too, in our spiritual lives our paths converge. Our stories overlap. They are the "stuff" that makes possible a dialogue, and, I hope, a way forward to better understanding the Lord's Prayer.

The Our Father is the only prayer that Jesus taught us. We might even say that he came to earth simply for this purpose: the Our Father. He was even put to death because he "called God his own Father, making himself equal with God." In the presence of the sheer mystery of God, we are all infinitely tiny. His mystery flowing over and around us is unimaginable and ineffable. We walk gropingly, by faith and not by sight. The path of prayer is steep and at times cold and rough. We stumble. John of the Cross says that on this path there are many "nights." The Lord's Prayer transforms our desolation—whether in prison or outside. We are given direction and freedom. Through the power of God, bad news is turned into good news.

The prayer offers a healing, a message and a preferred way of adoration. I view the Our Father as a shelter, providing security for all the scarred and bruised people of the world. But the depths of the Lord's Prayer can never be plumbed; it transcends our powers of imagination. Nevertheless there is nothing we cannot achieve if we seek out its meaning, if we keep its company.

We speak the words of the Our Father so often that routine erects a barrier and keeps us from experiencing all its fruits. That has happened to me and continues to happen. It is necessary to constantly relearn this prayer and meditate on its divinely given wealth.

The plan I will follow in these pages is simple. I am not proposing an academic study of the prayer. I will go through the words of the Our Father attentively, phrase by phrase. The text I will use is the one from the Sermon on the Mount in chapter six of Matthew, a version with seven petitions, unlike the one in Luke, which has only five.

I use the word *petition,* but we can be even bolder than that. When Jesus spoke to us and gave us the Our Father, he used the imperative. He urged us to command with him. Under his direction, we "dare" to speak to the Father, we have the "courage" to pray and we can even "order" with power. Jesus' gift to us, the Our Father, is our most precious inheritance. That is why, in the early days of the church, the Our Father was the prayer of "full members" only. The others did not know it, did not hear it; they had left the church or gathering by the time this prayer was said in the mass.

We are "full members" when we collaborate with

Jesus, when we listen with a disciple's attention to the dialogue between our hearts and the word, when we allow the Holy Spirit to act, when we begin to experience God's boundless gift.

These reflections on the Our Father will give way to a description of Abraham House. An alternative to incarceration, the very heart of Abraham House is rooted in the spirit of the Lord's Prayer. At Abraham House prisoners are able to make that journey from relating to God as Our Father in hell to Our Father in heaven.

Our Father

If you become Christians, you start to know the Father.
Epistle to the Pagan Diognetus
A.D. 190

*T*he word *Father* appears 170 times in the Gospels. It would be enlightening to read the New Testament, pause every time we encounter the word, and ask ourselves what each passage reveals about Jesus and his Father. However, to avoid misconceptions, we must understand that when the word *Father* is applied to God, it carries no limitations and is not confined to our knowledge of human fatherhood. The fatherhood of God can easily be called the motherhood of God. God the Father is neither a human being nor a mythical entity. In the Lord's Prayer there is no reference to the human categories of woman and man. Each woman and each man is urged to look, not sideways at one another, but in the same direction—upward, and much further. When applied to God, the words *Father* and *Mother* converge, overlap and enrich each other. Even then, we never succeed in fully grasping their profound meaning, because they point to heaven.

In reference to God, the word *Father* keeps us from being anxious and paralyzed with fear. Of course, the Bible does insist in numerous passages on the immense distance between God and us: "...you cannot see my face; for man shall not see me and live" (Ex 33:20). When we consider the first phrase of this prayer, however, Jesus immediately offers us a relationship with a Father and with a Mother, all-powerful, yet gentle and all-loving. In God's presence we are able to stand forth just as we are. A parent—a mother, a father—is naturally loving. Even the animals cherish their offspring. We see that a newborn is protected, sheltered, given preference. So when the Bible speaks of the distance between God and us, it also reveals a tender affection and deep intimacy. The reality we experience in our families, in the best of them, gives only a faint image of the divine. Nevertheless the love found in the family—happy they who experience it and have seen it—is the truest and most real starting point for speaking about heaven.

French writer André Frossard relates a story about a grandmother who was raising her grandson. The child was constantly stealing. To the despair of his grandmother, no reproach had any power over him. One day, in exasperation, she laid hold of her grandson, drew him to the fireplace, heated a poker red-hot, and said to him: "If you steal again, I will pierce your hand with this poker." But the grandson just kept on stealing. The grandmother took this impossible child, pulled him to the fireplace, heated the poker red-hot and...pierced her own hand with it. From that time on the grandson never stole again.

In this story the grandmother takes on the punishment meant for her grandson. We see in this a reflection of the type of love Jesus has for us. In this love for us, there is no separation between Jesus and the Father. Jesus came to the earth to love us, taking on himself our whole burden, our human condition. His entire life was dedicated to revealing his Father, setting him before us and, if possible, winning our acceptance of him.

Throughout the Gospel, in everything said about Jesus, there is a revelation of the Father. That is the hidden jewel, the hidden pearl. The first recorded words of Jesus, in Luke 2:49, are those he speaks at the age of twelve when he is found among the teachers of the law. To his parents, who have been frantically searching for him, he has but one response: "Did you not know that I must be in my Father's house?" And again in Luke 23:46, his final words on the cross are: "Father, into thy hands I commit my spirit!"

Everything about Jesus inspires us to draw near to the Father. Just citing a few passages from Scripture points this out:

Matthew 7:21: "...but he who does the will of my Father who is in heaven."

John 7:16: "My teaching is not mine..."

John 8:28: "...I do nothing on my own..."

John 12:50: "...I say as the Father has bidden me."

John 14:9–10: "Have I been with you so long, and yet you do not know me, Philip? He who has seen me has seen the Father; how can you say, 'Show us the Father'? Do you not believe that I am in the Father and the Father in me?..."

Matthew 11:25–26: "I thank thee, Father...for such was thy gracious will."

I often think that the Gospel is simply a set of fragments, chunks of stars that have to be put back together. Everything is given to us in the Gospel; all the food we need for the journey is there. But this historical Jesus is so "marginal," so "paradoxical," so "unconcluded" that he forces us to labor, much like a prospector working a piece of land for gold or a starving person looking for bread.

Jesus is the key that opens the door to the ultimate meaning of life itself, which is none other than the bond that exists between Jesus and the Father. This bond permeates all his actions. He is not a perfectly programmed robot, but a lover responding to a lover. He spends the night in communion with his Father; he withdraws to his Father when the crowd gets the wrong idea about him and wants to make him king. His secret is again, and always, the Father, and his constant desire is to make the Father his gift to us; "…I am ascending to my Father and your Father, to my God and your God" (Jn 20:17). The Father, whom Jesus possesses by his nature, he offers to us as an inheritance.

On Rikers Island, where more than twenty thousand men and women are imprisoned, *father* is often a curse word. How many families' stories I have heard there, stories of fathers that can be summed up in broken hopes: "It was my father who had put me in prison." "My father left; I never knew him." "I have just found my father here in prison. I had not seen him since I was eighteen." "I love blood and brawls. I never had a father to teach me to live." How is it possible, under such conditions, to proclaim and offer the blessed words, "heavenly Father," when even the most tenuous relationship to a father is missing; when the sons and daughters of this prison world have no one to listen to, to follow, to thank? How is it possible to make the leap from these cages and these wounds to a God who wants to be close to us and make known the joy He has in store for us?

There are moments when I no longer know the answer, but often in the midst of hell, God waits for us. When we are confronted with seared and torn lives, our response may only be silence. Yet, there can also be a quality of presence. There is a story told about Mother Teresa, who spent her life tending to the poor of Calcutta, that demonstrates this quality. Having found a dying child on a Calcutta street and seeing a person nearby, she placed the precious bundle in his arms and said, in words that fight against despair: "Love this child!" Like her, we can never solve all the problems, but we can keep anger, hostility and bitterness from being used as the final solutions. The first word, Our, of the Our Father raises us out of the depths. We are no longer alone, wrapped in the solitude of death. This *Our* binds me to the plural, the blessed plural of the communal dimension. If I want to turn to God and honor His fatherhood and motherhood, I cannot bypass the brotherhood and sisterhood, the faith community that has chosen Jesus as its teacher and Lord.

The *Father* of the Our Father transforms us into a family, a real family safeguarded against failures. Our Father is far removed from cheap sentimentality and romanticism, yet he requires that we become his daughters and sons, his close companions in loving service and attention to others. In God's world there are no strangers but only brothers and sisters. "...You have one Father, who is in heaven...," Jesus tells us (Mt 23:8–12).

Today, when people are forcibly marginalized, on Rikers Island and elsewhere, today, when many are sick because they have lost their identity or are isolated and spiritually frigid, the light of the Our Father restores warmth. There are, then, no longer any hermetically sealed borders or degrading exclusions. When we say the Our Father in Africa, in the Americas, in Europe or anywhere else, we throw ourselves, all together, into the Father's arms, while accepting the implied obligation and responsibility of doing everything we can to help one another, to rescue one another from an evil inequality and from the deep wounds that God suffers in his members: the starving children in all the deserts of the world, the civil wars, the AIDS epidemic, the increase in social violence, the poverty of the homeless and the unemployed, the endless misfortunes of the innocent and the reality of human guilt and human responsibility as well.

The sense of abandonment is evident so often. On Rikers Island I encounter bruised hearts and dulled eyes. I have seen the face, for example, of a woman who was returning to see her imprisoned brother and who told me that she was totally empty, devastated and in a mental and spiritual prison of her own because of him. I have encountered the interrogation of prisoners. I am on trial with them. "You come in the name of God. Where is God? Show me! Where is His touch?" While said in frustration, it is often a cry for help.

As Jesus told us, "This kind cannot be driven out by anything but prayer" (Mk 9:29). Belief in the power of prayer is the only medication for all these diseases. By that I mean no disrespect for the power of reason and intelligence. The mystery of prayer is not magic or fantasy. Prayer is not a possession or a commodity. If that were the case, all that would be needed would be to buy and own a prayer as one owns a home. Prayer is not programmed; it is alive and totally dependent on a source over which we have no control. Father René Voillaume, of the Little Brothers of Charles de Foucauld, never spoke of "professionals" when it came to prayer. He spoke rather of "permanent practitioners" of prayer. Prayer is a leap over the abyss, a leap taken with loving confidence, amazing trust. There is no question of a profession, but only an adventure. And who can program an adventure in advance?

Prayer is a total engagement of ourselves and a chosen way of life leading to a love affair with God. In prayer there is always something elusive, unexpected and inexplicable:

a sudden peace, a feeling of complete openness, a recognition of the truth. I remember a man dying of cancer. I was struck by his gentleness as he welcomed me. He was so willing to talk about his life, about his alienated son, about his love for him. "But I was never able to tell him. Can you tell him for me? It is so painful!" I promised him and so much peace came after this. This was a very special moment of grace. My prayerful encounter with his son enabled him to let go of his resentments and forgive his dying father. As always, prayer was the means through which he was able to rise above himself.

When the Our Father is lived and prayed both in laughter and tears, it opens us to the deepest dimensions of our lives, even gives us, in a cosmonaut's words, "instant global consciousness." Indeed, the Our Father embraces all our sisters and brothers throughout the world. They all reveal a different facet of God's unfathomable riches. So all-inclusive is this prayer that there are saints who never got beyond the two words: *Our Father.*

Summary

In the Lord's Prayer, Jesus urges us to be forceful, to command his Father and ours.

The word *Father,* when applied to God, bears only faint resemblance to human fatherhood. It encompasses the motherhood of God as well.

In God's presence we can stand forth just as we are. Like the best earthly parents (whether human or animal), God protects, shelters and nurtures.

The love found in cohesive, loving families is an excellent starting point for reflecting on heaven.

In honoring God's fatherhood and his motherhood, we cannot bypass our brotherhood and sisterhood, the faith community.

The more we enter into the Gospel, the more we realize that Jesus came to us to reveal and give us the Father.

When we truly choose to pray the Our Father, we start an adventure, that of a relationship with God and with our human community.

Each morning remember: the Father is all-important.

WHO ART IN HEAVEN

Out of the depths I cry to thee, O Lord! Lord, hear my voice!

Psalm 130:1-2

...He looked down from his holy height, from heaven the Lord looked at the earth, to hear the groans of the prisoners, to set free those who were doomed to die....

Psalm 102:19-20

Call upon God who is your Father in Heaven.

Treatise on the Lord's Prayer
Saint Cyprian

A French philosopher once said that hell was easier to imagine and describe than heaven. For some people heaven is a pie-in-the-sky place. For others it is God's home, where he wants us ultimately to live. Because we do not know how to lift our eyes beyond what is already seen, because the only world that seems tangible is our own, we are stymied by the riddle. What must heaven be like? Our fruitless discussions about heaven are, indeed, never ending. Unbelieving voices claim that in seeking God and heaven we are seeking an escape from the real needs of the moment, that we are telescoping the human condition and manifesting signs of schizophrenia.

Certainly, there are fantasies and false dreams. A cheaply bought mysticism heads straight for sheer blissfulness at the cost of reality. What Jesus offers when we pray and acknowledge his Father WHO ART IN HEAVEN is a broad and expansive understanding of heaven. It is not a material place; it is beyond everything and contains everything because it is God himself. The reality of God is called heaven. The fullness of life is there, far fuller life than on earth. It is a place of joy and of peace, where each of us can find what is most desired.

As we see in the lives of followers of Jesus, heaven provides a center, a secure base, a compass to guide their thoughts broader and more accurately "from God's point of view." It gives them a future and a new relative perspective on human folly. Evil cannot have the last word. The suffering of the world cannot be eternal. It lasts but a few hours. As Jesus opens his heart to the disciples and makes them aware of the turmoil to come, he adds, full of compassion, "I have said all this to you to keep you from falling away" (Jn 16:1).

The God who comes to heal our wounds comes even in the face of the worst situation. We don't need much experience to realize that there are situations in which everything conspires to make us lose heart; living at Rikers is one of them. Living twenty-three hours a day in a tiny cell, being subjected to a degrading routine of suspicion and control, no longer knowing what the words *dialogue* and *human dignity* mean—these experiences seemingly leave room only for nothingness or animality, the sort I witnessed one day in a cell block when an inmate was stabbed twelve times. I do not excuse real guilt by exercising the easy freedom of a passerby giving no thought to a brutal act. I do not forget the many victims of crimes or the wicked, who make prisons necessary. But more than once I was struck by something else. So often I have sensed vast questions behind an affected confidence or a broken hope: "I have done and experienced everything, and nothing lasts." "My father has already spent eleven years in prison and has just gone back in. My mother is on drugs and cannot help herself. And here I am on Rikers Island." "I cannot read in the cell block. It's too dangerous for me. I have too many enemies here. I must always keep my eyes open and be on guard." "I am suffering more in prison than I did in Vietnam."

There are unbearable, demoralizing sufferings in everyday life. The daily encounter with evil, whether in prison or in life outside, I call hell. Teilhard de Chardin put it another way: "A day is not far off when humanity will have only two choices, either suicide or adoration." That quote immediately came to mind on Christmas Eve 1995 when I was watching the TV news. That night the major story concerned a mass suicide by a sect in France. Indeed, where was joy to the world? And yet even with all our hellish experience of evil, the good, the good news of Christmas hope can never be extinguished. Two thousand years ago Paul sought to reassure us: "I consider that the sufferings of this present time are not worth comparing with the glory that is to be revealed to us" (Rom 8:18). He called us to become citizens of heaven. If we do, we can gradually overcome our sense of loneliness, our solitude, and we will no longer feel exiled.

We have some idea about heaven because Jesus talked about it. Because of him we are able to imagine it. Heaven was a familiar world for Jesus, a reality as profound and undeniable as our world. We learn from Jesus that the Father wants the blessedness of a union with him to be ours: "If a man loves me, he will keep my word, and my Father will love him, and we will come to him and make our home with him" (Jn 14:23). He possessed the secret of the kingdom of God.

In the hell that can be ours on earth, we lose our bearings. But the Father in heaven seeks union with us here on earth and is ready to help. The important word to remember is *union*. Without it, we are alone, each of us hopelessly struggling. Jesus invites us to seek union with the Father and each other. We are brothers and sisters, the children of our Father. As a priest friend of mine used to say: "A psychologist can define a loving person. But he cannot explain people loving one another." In other words, our very desire for union and mutual love is a revelation, a gift of God.

In New York I know many people who share my journey

and are saturated with the surrounding wretchedness of social ills. There are groups within the parishes who are open to the poorest and most alienated; and other groups who are the agents of unity, transcending race and social circumstance. These people speak of what is universal, of the great treasure all religions have in common: a fraternal, compassionate attitude toward the poor. But more often, I encounter a kind of misplaced compassion for any ministry to prisoners. My job is regarded as a dead-end street, second-rate pastoral care. "Why spend your time on the wicked?" "Who wants to be a chaplain over there when so many parishes are looking for priests?" "I would hate to be in such an environment." As a prison priest I notice how many people "outside" want to avoid, at any price, contact with the prison world. The public lends only a distracted ear to anything having to do with prison, even to the people speaking with the best intentions about alternatives to debilitating incarceration. And if the public actually listens, the listening quickly gives rise to a loud, aggressive outcry as soon as the community is asked to foot the bill for such alternatives or permit such a program in its midst. "Not in my backyard." At such moments, society simply refuses to see the obvious. Like it or not, prisoners someday will return as instruments of devastation, like the foxes that Samson set afire, tail to tail, among the enemies of his people (Jgs 15:3–5). What will be our reaction when they howl that they have never been given a chance?

Unfortunately, it happens that in some Christian circles an attitude toward prison ministry is not always as open, gracious and compassionate as I think I have a right to expect. Too rare is the cardinal such as Carlo Maria Martini of Milan, who explains, "When I begin my pastoral visitation to the archdiocese, I begin not with a visit to the cathedral, but to the prison. In this way I want to call attention to the importance of this form of ministry." A bishop, whose name I have forgotten, put it this way, "If I had only two priests in my diocese, I would make one of them chaplain in the Carmelite monastery and the other chaplain in the prison." That bishop was trying to say that in extreme places, we might even say places of excess, we can find astonishing resources of strength. We can even find there the antidote for all that ails humanity.

In conclusion, for all of us pilgrims, we can only attain the vast horizon of heaven by our complete openness, by giving the whole space of our life to God. All the Rikers Islands of this world might be considered places of hopeless alienation and even the trash cans of society, but they are the very places where God's word resounds. They are the very places that cry out to "Our Father who art in hell."

Summary

What Jesus gives us when we acknowledge his Father WHO ART IN HEAVEN is an understanding of heaven not as a material place but as God himself.

An awareness of heaven gives us a new perspective on human folly and suffering. The world, beautiful and tragic, is not the end of everything; it lasts but a short time.

We can look upon evil, and our daily experience of it, as hell. But if we only look at evil, we will lose our bearings. True joy and true peace are not out of reach even for people surrounded by hell. We are invited to seek union with Our Father, who is in heaven, and with each other. In the end we are all brothers and sisters, the children of Our Father.

HALLOWED BE THY NAME

It is good to give thanks to the Lord,
to sing praises to thy name, O Most High...
Psalm 92:1

God's Name is blessed when we live well,
but is blasphemed when we live poorly.
Sermon 71
Saint Peter Chrysologus

*I*n a very beautiful chapel of the religious of Graymoor, near Garrison, New York, there is a towering banner that glows with multicolored shapes of fire and flames. The banner hangs over a well-lit altar and represents Moses' vision of the burning bush. As the Exodus story goes, Moses has led his flock to Mount Horeb and suddenly finds himself near a bush that is burning. An encounter takes place there and a mysterious dialogue in which he receives the mission to lead the chosen people of God out of slavery in Egypt. Not only does Moses receive a mission, he also learns the identity of his mysterious partner in dialogue, the Name that will make his way down the centuries and is the beginning of an ever more detailed revelation: "I AM WHO AM." "Say this to the people of Israel, 'I AM has sent me to you....The Lord, the God of your fathers...has sent me to you': this is my name forever, and thus I am to be remembered throughout all generations" (Ex 3:14-15).

Our Jewish brothers and sisters refuse, out of respect, to utter God's Name. They even write "G-d," lest the paper upon which this word is written become torn or soiled and the Name of God blasphemed. In the Bible, as elsewhere, a name can convey many things. It can express a person's role—for example, *Abraham*, which means "father of a multitude"; or the meaning of an event—such as *Babel*, which means "confusion." In the case of God, the name YAHWEH emphasizes his power: I AM. The name also makes God present. It enables us to reach him, acknowledge him and become close to him in prayer.

I remember a Rikers prisoner coming to ask: "Father, can you pray for my daughter?" "Yes," I assured him, "but what is her name?" "I forget," he said. Naturally I felt sorry for the man and his daughter, yet that incident has often made me reflect with gratitude on how God never forgets any of our names. In prison names are replaced by numbers. Anonymity and a faceless mass are the rules. A person's official identification is a number. Because of this, nicknames abound: "Little," "Fat," "Shorty," "Hollywood" and so on. As in all caricatures, individuals are known by their most obvious traits and, alas, those most lacking in "spirit." The final tragedy is to die on Rikers Island, having given the authorities an alias. These men have no identity and are totally unknown; the authorities cannot inform anyone outside about the death. To a false name and false address is added the oblivion of burial in Potters Field on Hart Island, New York; the loss in human terms is now complete. All that is left is God's remembrance and mercy. For in his sight there is no incomplete file, no unidentified soul.

Every prayer is permeated with the Name, and depends on it. "Our help is in the name of the Lord" (Ps 124:8). "From heaven the Lord looked down at the earth ...that men may declare Zion in the name of the Lord" (Ps 102:19–21). "You shall not take the name of the Lord your God in vain" (Dt 5:11). "God has highly exalted him and bestowed on him the name which is above every name" (Phil 2:9). "...a sacrifice of praise to God, that is, the fruit of lips that acknowledge his name" (Heb 13:15). His Name is a treasure, one to be called upon earnestly. If we do not call God by name, we get mired in mediocrity, we

28

remain outside, and we are nothing but strangers. Left on our own, we know nothing, and thus idols become important. We no longer know what life is. And as a result, we die for lack of direction and light.

Here I could add text after text, page after page of anecdotes about the encounters I have had that illustrate this sense of utter confusion. One man told me, "There are times when I am afraid, times when I am full of doubts. I can be very malicious and act badly. I no longer believe in anyone: women, men, lawyers, judges, priests....I do believe, however, that I am searching for God. I wish I had something inside me, a seed that could grow and could help me. Why are the many people who speak of God so strange?" At Rikers the multiplicity of religions is often more daunting to seekers of truth than their basic disbelief. If you dig deep in most people's hearts, you find that they want an answer; they want to find God. The religious factor in people may be warped, but it is there; it exists.

I have witnessed this amalgam of religious searching, confusion, forgetfulness and derision in the prison ward at Bellevue Hospital, when a man was dying, while all around the inmates watched as a television spouted rubbish. I also sensed this at Rikers Island one morning after mass when a man came to the sacristy. His eyes were dull and glaring, yet he spoke clearly. He begged me: "Kill me, Father, kill me!" What was going on inside him? What ulterior motive or simple despair made him choose a priest as the person who might be willing to finish him off? Outside the door, corrections officers were urging other inmates back to their cells. I could only look at the man. That morning I left the prison, begging heaven for answers.

The only way to escape such despair is to jump into the Lord, to seek his shelter, his care. To call him by Name.

Only then can we find hope in our wounds. "The sacrifice acceptable to God is a broken spirit; a broken and contrite heart, O God, thou wilt not despise" (Ps 51:17).

The unique and most wondrous aspect of the divine Name is that it is Holy. "And holy is his name" (Lk 1:49). Just before his passion, when Jesus asks the Father to "glorify thy name," thunder is heard (Jn 12:28–29). That is the explosive force of God, his seal on what is coming. The glory and the Name are dynamic, charged with unimaginable power. And it is precisely thanks to this Name that the apostles and disciples "explode" with power and are able to expel demons and to heal: "I have no gold and silver, but I give you what I have; in the name of Jesus Christ of Nazareth, walk" (Acts 3:6).

HALLOWED BE YOUR NAME is the first petition of the Lord's Prayer, the first priority Jesus set forth as urgent. The words are not a simple disinterested wish; they are to be said as when we take an oath, and they should be given preference over everything else. Jesus has us begin at the highest level, with our eyes fixed on the goal. The higher we go in climbing a mountain, the more open space we see and the more insignificant details become. Jesus wants us to realize in our hearts what is more important. Our burdens, the details of life, suddenly are lighter and have a limited, relative impact on us.

We will never know how to get back to the Source if we remain occupied with pious trifles and distractions. Centered on ourselves, we inevitably muddle the message. On the contrary, we are meant to go out to him before turning to ourselves. In him we pass through the door of liberation, identifying our salvation, the Name that saves. In this way we become masters of our lives.

To pray that God's Name be hallowed or sanctified is to

know what holiness is, to desire to be associated with it. Speaking of his disciples, Jesus prayed to his Father: "...keep them in thy name which thou hast given me, that they may be one, even as we are one" (Jn 17:11). Jesus seeks to create an order of nobility, a new kind of personhood. Here there are no faceless masses, no demoralizing alienation, no one who is just a number, as in prison. Rather, we make the bracing discovery of our responsibility to each other before God. We are destined to connect and be in harmony with all the daughters and sons of the one Father.

Perhaps the words that best explain this sense of family are found in Jeremiah 15:16: "Thy words were found, and I ate them, and thy words became to me a joy and the delight of my heart; for I am called by thy name, O Lord, God of hosts." And in Jeremiah 14:9: "Yet thou, O Lord, art in the midst of us, and we are called by thy name." A Name, a Power from heaven is upon us. This is the most satisfying possession that can be given to us. But it is impossible for the proud to find this Name. We must approach the One who is at the heart of silence, the source and center of all, with humility, barefoot like Moses, "the humblest of human beings" (Nm 12:3).

To call for the sanctification of God is to be ourselves called, ready to work to help build a world in which everyone is important and has a place. It means saying an unconditional yes to the architect who owns the universe. Then human prisons, these places of extreme loneliness and darkness, become nothing but houses of cards. For when sanctification becomes our goal, we are able to transcend even the limitations of place.

As a chaplain I am convinced of the urgent and therapeutic power of an atmosphere. In prisons everything is cold, gray, alien, anonymous, brutal and noisy. Life stops: dreams stop. Flowers, light, color and worship are valuable means of achieving a rebirth in the Source. A place that provides repose, peace and beauty for the eyes becomes a place where God gives signs to people, a place of adoration and prayer. A chapel in prison is like one elsewhere. It is a place where it is quite normal and natural to turn from the trite to the essential, to kneel, to be silent...and find.

A request to bring the "sacred" into prison is the kind of issue that our legal system has difficulty handling. But sixteen years of experience has shown me the justification for the sacred in prison. On Rikers, from time to time, there are rumors that our chapel is to be eliminated "for the sake of more important needs." This would be an atrocity: the authorities do not know that they would only worsen their problems. In every human being there is an immense need to adore. Because of the illusions the world creates, life is often spent suppressing this need. We are all endangered masterpieces, at risk of losing our identity. Rebounding and finding our way again go hand-in-hand with finding God. The setting and the manner, though not absolutely necessary for the divine winds to "blow where they will," have their value. A chapel can transform despair into hope.

A commanding officer, on the eve of his retirement after more than twenty years in the Department of Correction at Rikers, confessed his regret and his powerlessness, as though in defeat: "In the beginning, when I first came here, I was sure that I would be able to change something in prison. Now, after what I have seen and am still seeing, I know that nothing can be done." Another high-ranking prison official expressed his frustration in similar words:

"In such a system, a person alone can do nothing. You are too confined by rules and regulations. I decided to try to climb in the system because I saw so many idiots above me. If they made it, I could too." Still another officer told me: "Every day that I come here, I want to leave immediately. But I have a family and this is the only work I have been able to find."

Must prison always end in failure? Is it the hopeless rock of Sisyphus? How can we get it into our minds and hearts that "nothing in this world can separate us from the love of Christ"? We would do well to travel the road that leads to the sacred, to the world in which the human is religious and the religious, human. The sacred is found in respect for the Name, and respect is what compels us to emerge from being self-centered, from shutting ourselves off. Instead, we become receptive and say, "Thank you." This sacred can be found on the physical level or in the "infinite spaces" of which Pascal, the French philosopher, spoke.

I believe I have touched this sacred, both in prison and far away from prison, during long, wonderful nights under the star-filled heavens of the Sahara. The brilliance, the silence, the isolation, the movements of countless stars, the universe of great distances, all compelled me to think "long and hard." A man in the desert said to me: "Here you become either a saint or a spiritual wreck." It is easy to lose perspective in the desert, with its bitter extremes, and where one feels powerless. Like the experience of our ancestors four thousand years ago in the Sinai wilderness, we wonder how not to crave "for the fish we ate in Egypt for nothing, the cucumbers, the melons, the leeks, the onions, and the garlic" (Nm 11:5). Yes, we can crave these things, but the people of the desert also learn the beauty of simplicity, of what is essential. While I was there I somehow understood why the people who live in deserts are spontaneously religious. There is no way for them to put life in perspective unless they come to grips with the infinite, moving into the inexhaustibly mysterious. Disciplined wills turn people into silent listeners, people of deep acceptance and real love.

I remember encountering a Muslim who had truly been a lord of the desert, with two hundred camels. Then he lost them all from disease, all his possessions. Even so, his face remained peaceful and he welcomed our small group with eggs cooked in burning ashes. He poured us mint tea. He had become poor, like Job, and was always praying on his rosary the ninety-nine names of God, among them "the Merciful," "the Compassionate," "the Almighty," "the First," "the Last." His worn-out tent, like the misery we many times encounter in prison, was a temple.

When we encounter such people so eager to call on God by Name, what a blessed experience! Everything around them seems to fall into place, into perfect harmony. It takes a long time to be able to say truthfully to God—or indeed to anyone—"I love you." Sometimes it takes a lifetime.

We can train ourselves to seek the sacred; it will be the door leading to our true selves, to others, and to God. In entering the universe of God, we should not lose heart, but instead lose our absurdity and despair. We may even become "enthusiastic." The etymology of the Greek word *en-theos*, mean "in God." To be in God is to be vigorous and healthy. Of course, it is difficult to remain "enthusiastic" throughout a lifetime; the reign of darkness never ceases assaulting our best efforts. Though our sins are not all the same, we are all responsible. In prison, I often say that we each depend on one another, both for good and for evil. Just as evil multiplies evil, so good multiplies good. Both alone and together we are challenged to experience the mystery of God's holiness. This is the experience Isaiah had when he was overwhelmed by his awareness of the difference between himself and God: "Woe is me...for I am a man with unclean lips" (Is 6:5). It is also the experience that comes when reading the words of the Psalm: "Be still, and know that I am God" (Ps 46:10), or when listening to Job: "I had heard of thee by the hearing of the ear, but now my eye sees thee; therefore I despise myself, and repent in dust and ashes" (Jb 42:5-6).

The life of heaven, that which the Bible calls "rest" in God, has nothing in common with the pallid and often meaningless character of what we on earth call "reality." To learn of the life of heaven and to stammer of it a little in adoration is not to engage in a naive dream; it is rather to find a childlike and yet utterly certain path that enables us to walk through fire. Now.

And to return to the heart of what I have tried to say in these pages: the word of God must not lead us back to fantasies. It contains the fullness of life and obliges us to acknowledge it. His Name says it all as we can read the poster in the chapel of the House of Detention for men at Rikers:

> I was regretting the past
> And fearing the future.
> Suddenly my Lord was speaking:
> "My Name is I AM."
> He paused. I waited. He continued:
> "When you live in the past

With its mistakes and regrets,
It is hard. I am not there.
My Name is not "I was."
When you live in the future
With its problems and fears,
It is hard. I am not there.
My Name is not "I will be."
When you live in this moment
It is not hard. I AM here.
My Name is I AM."

Summary

The command: HALLOWED BE THY NAME prompts us to start high, with what is most important. Jesus encourages us to fix our eyes on our goal.

God's Name emphasizes his power: "I AM."

We can train ourselves to seek the sacred; it will be the door leading to our true selves, to others, and to God.

To call for the sanctification of God is to be ourselves called (from our self-centeredness) to work for him.

The only way to find direction, identity against all despair, is to call on God by Name with awe and respect. Then our absurdity melts away. We lose our individuality and become one with him:

"I—with you—AM."

THY KINGDOM COME

...the kingdom of God does not mean food and drink but righteousness and peace and joy in the Holy Spirit.
Romans 14:17

...I see that sin—my sin and the sins of others—darkens the life of your Bride the Church.
Saint Catherine of Siena

*I*n the Gospel of Matthew, it is written: "From the days of John the Baptist until now the kingdom of heaven has suffered violence, and men of violence take it by force" (Mt 11:12). For me these words are a call to act with force, to move, take charge and fully cooperate with Jesus to make the kingdom come. The people in the Gospels who fail most are those who do nothing and the Lord is clearly impatient with them.

A monk is a person whose life is a protest, someone shouting in silence a no to idols, the false values and distorted priorities of the world. In the early centuries after Christ, when there were no longer any martyrs because the church was officially accepted, some Christian men and women began to renounce and leave behind the artificiality and excessive materialism of society. Theirs was a radical step to overcome the evil in the world by confronting it first within themselves. They were like the people whom Moses led and who, over the course of forty difficult years, learned to stake their lives on God. The desert fathers with their teacher, Saint Anthony, the Benedictines, Franciscans, Cistercians, Carthusians and countless others, exemplify this protest that takes the form of leaving behind the secularized world that has forgotten its true destiny.

These monks, these early Christian men and women, have continued to be lighthouses for us throughout the ages. No matter where we are or what we do in the world, we can look to these men and women to better understand the kingdom. By their lives they demonstrate that the way we believe is often as important as what we believe. Monks do not reject the world—actually just the opposite. They believe they can effect change in the world by how they live.

Today's deserts are not usually places of sand like those Anthony and his monks knew, but any place where humans, particularly the poor, gather. They are places like the South Bronx, where pastoral care and the prophetic work of evangelization take the form of struggling "to do justice, and to love kindness, and to walk humbly with your God" (Mi 6:8). There is a common goal between the monk and the person living and working in today's deserts—both are hoping, asking, praying, working that the kingdom come. Both have dedicated themselves to that same dynamic awakening and reawakening. When the kingdom comes to us, it is God himself who comes, to transform our thoughts, hearts and very lives. The kingdom is the reality of God himself, and we are asked to share with him, as inadequate guests, indeed, but as people nonetheless intimately called. We have been made for God, and when we forget him, we go astray and are "restless," as Saint Augustine says. All of us are called to embark upon the same apprenticeship of serving the kingdom.

This kingdom was made known and explained by the prophets. "I saw in the night visions, and behold, with the clouds of heaven there came one like a son of man....His dominion is an everlasting dominion, which shall not pass away, and his kingdom one that shall not be destroyed" (Dn 7:13-14). Along with this revelation about the kingdom a promise was also made: "The kingship dominion and the greatness of the kingdoms under the whole heaven shall be given to the people of the saints of the Most High" (Dn 7:27). This message is intended to help us understand the nature of true happiness; it is a message of hope for the darkest hour, like a lamp lit at nightfall.

When Jesus came, he began his mission with this proclamation: "The time is fulfilled, and the kingdom of God is at hand..." (Mk 1:15). The presence of the kingdom is later closely identified with the presence of Jesus: "...the kingdom is in the midst of you" (Lk 17:21). Thus the kingdom is not so much a place that can be marked on some map of the universe, but an event that touches everything that exists. From the beginnings of the biblical account down to our day, the kingdom has been the ultimate goal.

The kingdom is uniquely important and it requires a complete change of heart if we are to approach and enter it. To accept it by a total conversion is to emerge from darkness: "...if it is by the Spirit of God that I cast out demons, then the kingdom of God has come upon you" (Mt 12:28). The kingdom, then, is God's plan, his intention, his will for the world. A better quality of life is precisely what Jesus offers us. Where Jesus is, there is the kingdom. He offers the kingdom to the apostles and to all who will later believe in him: "...as my Father appointed a kingdom for me, so do I appoint for you" (Lk 22:29). The kingdom is a pure gift, extended magnanimously to all the world.

A careful reading of the Gospel shows that by the end of his life Jesus had taught us everything we need to know about the kingdom: how to look for it and to find it. His lessons range from the description of the seed in the field (Mt 13:24), to the certainty of a reward for the poor in spirit and those persecuted for justice's sake (Mt

5:3–10), to the demanding but absolutely necessary practice of compassion (Mt 25). To seek the kingdom above all else is the necessary condition for gaining everything (Mt 6:33). The preface of the mass of Christ the King, the final feast of the liturgical year, celebrates this great gift in a short formula that is long in meaning: "A kingdom of truth and life, a kingdom of holiness and grace, a kingdom of justice, love and peace." The kingdom is a gift through which Jesus asks us to work with him "so that the world may believe."

A practical example of openness to the kingdom occurred in a place where I lived for three unforgettable years. In the valley bottoms of Virginia and Kentucky, as the road ends the suffering begins. I saw illness, misery and powerlessness of every kind; brutalized lives, concealed wounds, hidden forms of poverty. Yet, in the midst of all that, I also saw glimmers of hope, through the loving presence of so many dedicated people, such as the Glenmary missionaries. The church was an active presence, with priests, brothers, sisters and lay volunteers reaching out in a "barefoot ministry." These men and women were filled with passionate hope and determination to counteract all the negativity and to proclaim in every situation that God had not abandoned his children.

Pastoral workers in prisons are often astonished to find these paths of transformation being traveled by inmates. To make the kingdom come, each of us has to find his or her own way. For some people, this means working professionally to change society. For others, it is to lift up perhaps only one other person....In neither case can we afford to be self-satisfied or simply resign ourselves to the status quo.

To be effective, compassion is not enough. We need

courage, vision, action—and with all that, respect for the uniqueness of the people we want to help. We need to help them come to know themselves and take responsibility for their own lives. My friend, the father abbot of the trappist monastery in Berryville, Virginia, told me quite unaffectedly (he was thinking of prisoners and especially those condemned to a lengthy punishment): "Tell them that their future here on earth lasts but a second, but they can already begin to live another life that will last forever." Another monk urged me to tell them "to transform their cell into a hermitage." These men were not trying to sell dreams or fantasies to souls crushed by abandonment and affliction. They were men in love with long and very difficult prayer, brothers who, along with their no to the world, want to speak to others of a treasure and destiny that we all have in common.

An urgent and haunting appeal for the kingdom rises up out of situations of suffering and darkness. "The hardest moment of the day for me is the moment of waking in the morning and finding myself here," one Rikers Island inmate told me one morning. This man carried with him, written on his face, immense failure. He talked of his constant desire to sleep. As a child, he had been tied up by his father and left under the kitchen sink. He had no friends; they all abandoned him. The mother of his two children was psychologically and morally fragile. He was haunted by the thought of losing her. He then went from his own situation to that of the world and linked his lot with that of the multitude of imprisoned people. With what he saw in our world—the inequalities and frustrations, even in the midst of wealth, the abject poverty and so forth—he knew that most people were sick at heart. He said: "The more I reflect on it, the more I think that at least 90 percent of the people are also in prison. Their lives are fettered by countless things."

In prison ordinary life does not exist. Or rather, what is ordinary is abnormal to those outside. One prisoner told me: "I have no fear of God. In my case I listen to nobody but myself. To kill is nothing for me. I just think about myself." Prison is a concentrated human jungle; and this anti-kingdom renews itself day after day. Crisis reigns. It is a hell of anger, where everything is important but the importance of life itself. Although there are societies for the protection of animals, there is so little for the protection of human beings.

When a ship sinks in the ocean, the sight is spectacular. How striking are the photographs—and the film—of the Titanic. There is turmoil, confusion—people in flight and fighting for life. But after the sinking, waves erase everything. There is nothing to see, not one trace left. It is as if nothing had happened. Only the sea remains. In jail, much the same thing happens. There is a fatal fight in a cellblock or a suicide in a cell. And afterward, after the report has been dutifully made, a sanitation crew mops up the blood on the floor. There is no mourning, no official comment. The only remembrance perhaps are prayers in the chapel. The jail remains.

In the face of such horror, the only true relief is the joy that comes from living in the kingdom. It is a precious, hard-earned joy. This perhaps explains why the bishop I mentioned singled out Carmel and prison as places where the church must be visibly implanted. In both, nature rebels and faith makes its way with struggle, with a change of attitude, with the "vertical path," as John of the Cross would put it. Against the insidious and sometimes alarming incubation of evil, another way is needed that can direct the will and transform the vision from tearing down to building up, from chaos to harmony, from chains to freedom. In short, from the kingdom of anger to the kingdom of God.

Indeed, I have seen the kingdom coming at Rikers through the very words of the prisoners themselves: "When I pray I am in shape." "In the past, I didn't go to mass. Now I am anxious to go." "God, I give my soul, but without any guarantee on my part. Keep it with you." And on Ash Wednesday a prisoner asked me: "I am going to court today. Please give the ashes to my brother. He is incarcerated here. And he will give them to me when I come back from the court." Such words, in a place where everything seems lost, are the result of countless graces. His kingdom is truly coming. Our work and his gift meet.

When we talk about the kingdom, the visible elements may be relative, but still the true kingdom compels us to touch and experience, to enter into the "come and see" of the Gospel. The kingdom is Christ's message and also Christ as messenger; it is the person of Jesus we constantly seek and serve. This includes all the tender love and ongoing compassion of the Son of God, which is also the reality we call the church. If there is complete accord among what Jesus says, what he does and what he is, there is also a solid, unavoidable connection among the kingdom, Jesus and the church—both the church in heaven and the church on earth. Each of us is born with our own parochialism, and our biases and prejudices only seem to increase with the passage of time. But even so, we can experience well-founded certitudes in our lives and at certain moments even touch the truth.

I am personally convinced, for example, of my need to

belong to the church on earth. This certitude I have dis-
covered and regard as precious and grace-filled, even
though many people today have their own personal reasons for questioning, challenging or rejecting the church.
As an ordinary human in constant need of forgiveness,
one who is allergic to emptiness and cold and has no
patience for violence, I have learned to love and cherish
the faith of the church—from the faith in the small town
in France where I was born to the faith in New York. This
faith is "the one thing necessary" of which Jesus speaks.
It gives perspective to everything. Without any merit on
my part, I have advanced some little way in this faith. I
have no lessons to teach anyone, but can at least trust in
the experiences that have formed me and brought me to
this point.

It seems to me quite obvious that I ought to love my
church, even amid sufferings she causes, has caused and
still causes the world. In church history we inevitably find
mistakes, liabilities, even evil, all of which are as real in
the church as is her holiness. The stains of the Crusades
and the Inquisitions, two appalling movements, come to
mind, as do others much closer to our time. But who am I
to raise my head against the church and incite people to
cry scandal? I cannot reduce the church to what I see and
know or to what concerns me individually.

The weakness of any family—including the Church—
belongs to all the members. When the family is bound
together in truth, all the members share the burden of
their weakness and take it to heart equally. While there
are outward appearances, there is also a heart. Nothing
can change the fact that the church continually gives to
the world that inexhaustible gift of Christ, the eucharist.
With all her rough spots and thorns, she embraces the

luminous Christ and a broad spectrum of luminous witnesses. Their crosses and their glory are always present.

The church, in her long history, has mistreated human beings and caused blood to flow, nonetheless it is in her that the privileged sign of the kingdom is given—the good news is preached to the poor. The church is the place where we are trained to love and where we can catch a glimpse of the kingdom. The church of the martyrs and saints is no figment of the imagination. As Kenneth Woodward writes, the "...church is unthinkable without sinners and impossible to live without saints."

To leave the church because of accidents along the way would be to stifle my own breathing. There is worldliness in the church, there is aridity, darkness, indifference and injustice, but empty bitterness is not a viable reaction. In the kingdom of God, the energy of God is at work, and the church cannot be reduced to an uncomfortable waiting room that leads to some ethereal kingdom beyond. Even with her wrinkles, even with her unfulfilled responsibilities, which are surely shared by all, burdened as we are to the end by original sin, she still represents our greatest hope.

When we pray at mass: "Look not upon our sins but on the faith of your church," we are siding with what is true. The faith is the church's faith. Our faith depends on hers. Yes, the church needs to be reformed, but by means of each person's tears and strength of soul. The impenetrable mystery of the cross is the only effective way to join together the rupture between a wounded, mutilated world and a seemingly unapproachable church. Perhaps that is the way it will be until the end. The journey from the Peter who denied Christ three times to the Peter who, finally, completely, magnificently dedicated himself to

Christ is perhaps emblematic of the church's journey. Although the church is established by God, she is always in the process of conversion, even in her most prominent members.

Today, the church needs to accept certain changes in a changing world, just as she needs to confront legitimate questions. But concerns about whether there is a God, whether he is with us to the end, whether a door is open to a kingdom—these are far more weighty, ultimate questions. I love the fidelity of the martyrs, who preferred injustice to blasphemy, the blasphemy of turning the church into an enemy. Evil is the enemy, and as the Gospel tells us, much in me and in us is evil. Whether I like it or not, the church is the branch that bears me up. Whatever I think or do, I will always be less than she. The future the church entrusts to us is the longest lasting of all; it is nothing short of eternity. For this very reason, in prison and everywhere else, the church counts. So, too, does her visibility. We all depend on her, and her absence from our lives would be suicidal. By listening and experiencing the word together as community—where two or three are gathered in his Name—we are reborn. Like everything that is put to the test of time, our sense of belonging to the church must be constantly renewed and celebrated.

Each day the church shows us the way to the kingdom. Each day she teaches us another lesson in wisdom and provides a new look at the meaning of life, at the meaning of success which is so different from the world's perception of success. The food given by the church is always available and plentiful enough for our needs. She leads us home to the kingdom where there will be no more idols.

Summary

Jesus inspires us to act forcefully with him to make the kingdom come.

Each of us makes the kingdom come as we discover our own contribution to the world. For some people this means working to change society. For others it means lifting up perhaps only one other person.

When the kingdom comes to us, it is God himself who comes to transform our very lives.

If there is complete identity and accord between what Jesus says, what he does and what he is, there also is a solid, unavoidable connection among the kingdom, Jesus and the church.

The process of reforming the church starts in our own hearts.

To put the kingdom of God above all else is the necessary condition for gaining everything (Mt 6:33).

THY WILL BE DONE ON EARTH AS IT IS IN HEAVEN

And the world passes away, and the lust of it; but he who does the will of God abides forever.

1 John 2:17

I am not interested at that time to be out of jail. I would just like to do the will of God.

A prisoner at Rikers

I remember someone asking: "How do you make God laugh?" The answer: "You tell him your plan." Whenever we try to take total control, our frantic efforts themselves become laughable. We would do better to ask, with the simple attitude of a child, what God's plan is for us. Just as a child runs home after school, exploding with life and laughter, eager to tell his parents what has happened that day and to find out their reaction, we want to do the same with the Lord. We want to share our needs with him and find out what his plan is for us. He is vitally interested in our lives and never leaves us alone. Jesus reminds us that we should not be anxious about our life (Mt 6:25). We receive shelter and security just by doing his will. Our true light and life come from outside ourselves. We are not the author. We simply receive.

To will what Jesus commands is surely to win heaven, for it means finding our place of refuge in him. As such, we learn to be detached from things and not to hold onto them as though we were their owners. If we unburden ourselves of things we can give the fullest possible welcome to reason and grace, which is where God is. In fact, to do what Jesus commands is to put ourselves in the position of expecting nothing less than miracles and wonders. It is to acquire an innocent, unique clear-sightedness that achieves the impossible, that makes the impossible possible, accessible, natural, even matter-of-fact. Why? Because such clear-sightedness is fully open to recognize and receive surprise after surprise. A bright melody, a skillful hand, a long fidelity, a skyscraper, a bunch of grapes, a sun setting ablaze on a summer evening, these are all miracles and masterpieces. It would be a shame if our eyes were so faded as to diminish reality or to turn life into a commonplace routine, a colorless indifference.

How truly wonderful to accept with our whole being, and keep alive within us, the words of Psalm 19: "The heavens are telling the glory of God." They tell it like a story for the eyes: a sparkling story full of light that gives joy to the heart. Just as the beauty of the universe shows forth the glory of God, so too does the beauty of each human being. Saint Irenaeus expressed this sublimely when he wrote: "The glory of God is the living human being, and the glory of the human being is the vision of God."

Jesus offers children as a model for us in seeking to do God's will. He says: "Be like them." He is not proposing nostalgia, but a goal, a permanently valid model. It is as if we were all born already old but are now encouraged and given the opportunity of another real and much richer birth. Children do not leave reality or reason behind when they wonder. Their intense excitement is pure, totally unalloyed. Their discovery does not leave them exhausted and does them no harm, as some misplaced enthusiasm would. If they fall, it is never from a great height, and they are always light, buoyant. They easily recognize and experience peace and joy. They "sense" things and differentiate very clearly among them.

A child once told me: "When I do not love, it seems to me that I am alone." People sense that they cannot lie to children, or tell them that they love them when they do not. Children need only look. Their life is a morning, a setting out, an endless game. They learn from the slightest thing by "transfiguring" it.

Two familiar photographs of the French adventurer and ardent convert to Christianity, Charles de Foucauld, illustrate the point of regaining childlike wonder. The photos are obviously from different periods of his life. One shows a heavy, expressionless visage, the other a bright, beaming face. In the first photograph he is a puffy, sated young man slumped in idleness and indifference. In the second, Foucauld is intensely present, eyes filled with a burning light. Between the two photographs a long, unique and infinitely valuable pilgrimage took place as in the lives of the saints. The mating of grace and humanity can transform a life just as it did Foucauld's before his murder by a subversive tribe in the Sahara desert on the first of December 1916. During his life Foucauld had moved from his agnostic exile into joyous union with God.

As we see with this noble man of God, the great theme of exile seems to be a constant in God's teaching, as he seeks to lead the human race to its final dwelling, heaven. The exile began with our father Abraham and turns all of us into people who are permanently dissatisfied with times and places in our journey through the wilderness toward the promised land. The word *passover* means "passage"— passage that began with the exodus from Egypt and continued down to the experience of the empty tomb on the morning of the resurrection.

Exile is a break, a disorientation, an experience of strangeness and wandering; it speaks more of waiting than of arrival, more of patience than of joy fulfilled. Precisely for this reason, exile can become the setting for an urgent and repeated invitation to intimacy with God.

"So we are always of good courage; we know that while we are at home in the body we are away from the Lord, for we walk by faith, not by sight" (2 Cor 5:6-7). "Beloved, I beseech you as aliens and exiles to abstain from the passions of the flesh that wage war against your soul" (1 Pt 2:11). "These all...acknowledged that they were strangers and exiles on the earth. For people who speak thus make it clear that they are seeking a homeland.... Therefore God is not ashamed to be called their God, for he has prepared for them a city" (Heb 11:13-16).

The entire Bible is a book of journeys and exiles, as we see in the active formation of God's people. Recall, for instance, the prayerful remembrance of Moses: "A wandering Aramean was my father; and he went down into Egypt" (Dt 26:5). Because of the one "who is and who was and who is to come" (Rev 1:4), nothing could be more dynamic, more progressive than the Bible. As God "passed" by Abraham, "passed" before Moses, and "passed" before Elijah, so he puts us in motion, on a pilgrimage, a passage in our apprenticeship for heaven. Naturally, there are moments when it is easy to set out, moved perhaps by a simple desire for change or because the grass in the next field seems greener. But whether we want to or not, we are meant to spend our lives setting out.

A priest once said: "I have been living in this one place for twenty years. But if you only knew the journey I have been on!" That active dynamism found in the Bible, at work, too, in our life history, is far from limited to the physical world. Although the realities of time, space and distance are necessary if we are to have some way of gauging our journey, the real issue here has to do with another reality: the reality of the interior landscape and its spiritual depth. That is what the priest was referring to when he spoke of his "journey." Augustine's words are as true today as they were in his time: "You made us for yourself, and our heart is restless until it rests in you."

The word *exile* resonates strongly for me. I have been to too many places in my life. Even if the word *home* in this situation has different meanings, even if our nationality is an accident of birth, there is nothing to keep me from going back and giving a special value to the faces and places that have left their mark on my life. Is it a blessing or a disadvantage of old age that we remember and take inventory? I know that I, like everyone else, have been conditioned, shaped, tilled as it were, and given directions by my early years. Those years were steeped in a particular culture, within a well-defined world with landscapes that, even in New York, I can only describe as marvelous (anyone who has visited the Gorges du Tarn, near Millau, France, will have no doubt of this). Nevertheless I learned very soon that there would be other horizons.

We may think we have arrived, reached the ultimate point, but there is always something more distant. On earth, the familiar never lasts forever, and I seemed always to realize this. Life is a mystery of astonishment, adventure and novelty. It is a mystery that dazzles us and takes us where we would never dare think of going. But an innate curiosity also urges us to investigate other points of view, to explore the immense diversity of our fellow human beings, and even to "take flight," the very idea that runs through the Bible, beginning with Abraham.

Personally, I had a need to know, to discern, to test my roots, lest, as Saint Paul says, I be tossed about by every wave. To realize, for instance, that had I been born at Beni Abbes in the Sahara, I would very probably be a

Muslim. Yet God, the truth, the whole of things, cannot be simply summed up as the product of a culture. There is an energy in the clash of origins and ways of life, and life in New York has certainly made me aware of this.

Strangeness is an everyday experience here. At such times, the past is far distant. Like Mephistopheles, I could lightheartedly apply to myself the saying, "Forgotten at home, unknown elsewhere; such is the lot of the traveler." That is a condition, far more serious, faced by millions today. To begin with, they never chose their exile. They are the fallout of economic and political situations. Wherever we turn, how can we avoid seeing the dramatic results of being in exile, of being the victims of people's immense inhumanity to other people?

We have a persistent desire, then, to go beyond all divisions and separations. A desire for what is essential, for what endures despite chaos, changes and departures. Eventually, we learn an invigorating fidelity that cuts to the center of things, the kind that can be summed up in a word, a breath, a glance. A fidelity that searches for God's will. We can let go of all other baggage—and it is precisely our exile that makes this possible.

Prisons are places permeated with exile and overwhelmed with frustrations, where everything seems calculated to make inmates lose heart. Can the words, "THY WILL BE DONE ON EARTH AS IT IS IN HEAVEN," penetrate the walls of a prison? If God is everywhere except in evil, then it is possible to find him on Rikers Island. Yes, I have seen him there as men have tried to do his will. Someone once said: "If you are able to see the invisible, you are able to do the impossible." It is God who gives these men hope and a way out of anger; in him they are able to rebound.

The very day my friend Andrew got out of prison, he

came to me. His first action was to run into the chapel and kneel. Then he took down a very beautiful cross that was on the wall, one made of enamel and silver, and began to clean it. He went to work with rags and polish for well over an hour. It was as if he wanted to let out, once and for all, his past frustrations, depressions and suicide attempts, as if he had something in his hand now that could give him true answers, the key to a new world, the address of home. I have never seen a person who wanted so much to express his willingness to move from anger to adoration.

The Bible and its many witnesses to the faith help us see how many unacceptable situations are transformed by an unexpected light. Our journey toward a fullness and intensity of life reveals a great mystery. We find that God is at work, especially and above all in our weaknesses; God shows himself there without warning us in advance, as he prefers forgotten, unexpected places. The poor who seek and ask are called "happy" in the Gospel. There is a kind of sanctification of the emptiness, the waiting and the ignorance that, in another context and seen from a different angle, would cause us to howl and blaspheme.

I heard an American politician once say: "Every saint has a past, every sinner has a future." In Rikers, and indeed outside, there is unredeemed evil; the sinner with a future is the one who has the guts to put his trust in the will of God. The striking thing about saints is that, despite everything, their eyes are fixed on God and his promises, revelations and messages. And their gaze is all the more intense because no protective screen hinders it, not even the screen of their virtues and good qualities. This gaze focuses on the Source, and that is enough. As Thérèse of

Lisieux said: "If I had merits, I would have despaired immediately." She understood very early that the "littleness" of her way was the best means of entering into the will of God and letting herself be transformed by it.

Do we not see a connection between the "night" of prison and the "night" of the spirit? While it would be unrealistic and quite naive to find evidence of such connection everywhere, the sweeping away in prison of many illusions and possessions brings out, with a clarity rarely found elsewhere, the value and freshness of the Gospel. As a volunteer who came to join our Christian community on Rikers said to me: "Here every word of the Gospel hits home! The words make themselves heard!" The moment when we hear the words of faith in all their naked truth is a most important one, for it is the blessed first step in living them.

In every exile or separation, even though many human bonds are broken and cannot be restored, there is, for those who want it, a way to permanence, rootedness and profound stability. Spiritualizing one's life means preserving in one's heart the certainty that God is effectively at work, even when everything is lost. This certainty is all the more present to the degree that it remains the only familiar link with the past. Believers, by grace from on high, continue to make faith the chosen motive of their lives. Their attention is focused less on details, particulars and incidentals of the journey. They do not worry over a future that some evil power may have in store for them. They are convinced that because of the fidelity of which the Bible speaks over and over again, God will always be their Master and will have the last word.

When we have experienced many "migrations" in our lives—seen many places, done many things—we find the most permanent aspect of our existence is the divine, provided our hearts cling to that. Our troubles continue to condition our behavior and will be with us to the very end. Yet God is not affected by the changes in us. Our yes to his work and his will, even in the midst of weakness and new beginnings, make him our friend forever.

In the chapel in the maximum security building, the old House of Detention, on Rikers Island, there are green plants around the altar and at the back of the church. They add an element of peace, life and brightness. They help people understand that what happens in the chapel transcends everything, even the routine toleration of the administration, which is obliged under state law to include within the walls of prisons a place of worship. One morning, Henry, an inmate of several months who has never missed mass, joyfully showed me new blossoms on the plants: "These have almost no fresh air. Nevertheless they find a way of producing blossoms. That's a good sign. We, too, lack air. They show that there is hope for us."

He had told me earlier that prayer helped him more than anything else in this place. It was clear he was not afraid, that his days in exile were filled with God and he was living in God. Another inmate said of Henry: "People like him create a new atmosphere for you." Though filled with courage and endurance, Henry did not deny his trials. But because he wanted God's will on his side, he was able to transform those trials. His was a school of peace and hope. Without knowing it, he too was producing flowers.

Summary

The sinner with a future is the one who puts his trust in the will of God.

We can be like children, sharing our experiences and needs with our Father. He will tell us what is best, what his plan is for us.

Giving up our will daily to the Father is a difficult, but transforming and liberating experience.

God is at work, especially through our weaknesses. The poor, who seek God with empty hands, will find them filled; these people are called "happy" in the Gospel.

Many times Jesus was unable to perform miracles because people were closed and unreceptive.

The entire Bible is a book of journeys and exile. When we have experienced many "migrations" in our lives— seen many places, done many things—we find the most permanent aspect of our existence is our longing for the divine, our faith.

Gradually we understand that the Father's will is at the core of our mission.

GIVE US THIS DAY
OUR DAILY BREAD

The Father in heaven urges us, as children of heaven, to ask for the bread of heaven. Christ himself is the bread who, sown in the Virgin, raised up in the flesh, kneaded in the passion, baked in the oven of the tomb, reserved in churches, brought to altars, furnishes the faithful each day with food from heaven.

Sermon 67
Saint Peter Chrysologus

Good news rarely gets good publicity. Even the history books emphasize wars and atrocities. Good news is not titillating or shocking. Supposedly, it does not arrest our attention. It is thought to be like water: colorless, odorless and tasteless. Current events rain down on us in a hail of negatives. "If you could wring out a newspaper the way you wring out a piece of cloth," an imprisoned friend said to me, "nothing would come out but blood. There is nothing there but war, crime and violence." In prison, too, it is disturbances or violence that rouse interest; people talk about them. But good news, touching our conscience, dignity or the rediscovery of a person's humanity, apparently stirs no one—or too few.

If even small bits of good news have so much trouble winning attention, the disregard of the BIG good news, which is meant to sweep away our fears, is surely understandable. It never will be possible for us to "sell" our experience of faith and everything connected with the word of God. There is no *Daily News* or *New York Times* for the Gospel. Individuals must each make the good news their own and accept the struggle, the grace, the wounds and the risks.

So often the media focus on illusions that have nothing to do with our real-life situations. I remember seeing a tramp stretched out in the sun on Eighty-sixth Street in Manhattan; lying on the pavement, he was leafing through the self-indulgent pages of *Interior Design*! Could anything be more incongruous than that scene? Could there be any greater distance between that man and what his eyes were seeing? In a real way we are all vagrants, begging God for our daily bread. The difference is that our divine Provider makes himself available, a fellow companion in our journey. Like Elijah journeying to Mount Horeb, we need nourishment for both body and soul to walk through our daily desert. But we always ask that God give US this day our daily bread. The words compel us as individuals to open our eyes and look further. We are a community of people, working each day to make the kingdom come in this world. Ours is a work in progress. Only in the end will the fullness of the kingdom exist.

God's gracious will looks on the community of Jesus, on those who follow him. Those who want to work with Jesus are assured of a quality and quantity of life from heaven. We need this to be totally alive. We need the resoluteness of the royal Magi, who despite the risks, set out on a lengthy journey because of a star. Their caravan came to a halt in an out-of-the-way, unimportant place where, disregarding all worldly measures of probability, they chose to worship a child in a stable. Yet the people who normally would have been the first invited to worship, because they knew the Scriptures and the promises and because they lived in Jerusalem, did not stir.

The message is clear: The good news can be received only by hearts that are prepared, wide open with expectation. But how are we to prepare ourselves for the good news here in the midst of our wretchedness, with all that is going on in the visible, immediate world, in the "theater" of our life? The answer lies in the prayer: "GIVE US THIS DAY OUR DAILY BREAD."

In the parable of the prodigal son we are told he "came to himself" (Lk 15:17). This is the moment of truth for the son, the moment of his reaching maturity before God. When we finally learn, after too many conflicts, failures and disasters, that we are neither masters nor lords (and our patient God shows us this even if it takes a whole life-time), that is precisely when the grace of a turning point comes, and then a radical new beginning. The one whom we call God can no longer be a superficial adornment, someone we take for granted, who has no impact on our lives. Like a seed in the ground, he often shows himself only at the end of a long, difficult and costly history. Then, at last, the totality of our lives is given direction.

In the eyes of God the realities that fill our lives—all the needs, joys, labors, cares, impoverishments—are very important. These we must bring before God; otherwise we may make the mistake of turning prayer into an escape or a vague final appeal when everything else has failed. "I have asked the Lord to watch my back. For the rest, I can take care of it," a prisoner told me. He was athletic, sure of himself and his abilities. I saw a similar message on a banner in the streets of Harlan, Kentucky, during the social upheavals of the '70s: "Pray for the dead, but fight like hell for the living." A more holistic approach to prayer covers every aspect of our lives, including our abilities as well as all those living around us.

We cannot carry the full weight of our cares while forgetting the teacher, Jesus the Savior, nor can we cast our cares wholly on the Lord without a sense of responsibility. The truth—and the mystery—lies in the expression, "Everything is God's gift; everything is man's task." Both commitment and detachment need to be constantly renewed in our daily life: "Work as if everything depended on us; pray as if everything depended on God."

The Our Father teaches us to temper our sense of self-sufficiency and practicality. We cannot buy the bread of life; we must ask God for it. We have to give God "permission," as Mother Teresa often said, to intervene in our lives. God wants to work for us, and he wants us to work less. He wants us to hear the Psalm (55:22), "Cast your burden on the Lord, and he will sustain you." And so put our worries in perspective.

Every morning I have to remember that the Father is all-important, that the reality of the human world has to be connected to another reality that is much more effective. The Lord is looking for my trust and my faith; he is waiting for my call. A monk once said to me: "Often it is when we can do nothing more that God works the hardest, because we have put ourselves totally at his mercy, in his hands." We have to dive into the emptiness with only the parachute of faith.

Each day we make our petition to God...GIVE US THIS DAY. We cannot postpone our prayer; the gift we seek is in the present. The Father's favor is here and now, like the "now" in the Hail Mary. Faith, trust and courage to advance—these are living realities to be rediscovered each morning as we rise from bed and address ourselves resolutely to the author of all gifts.

To pray is to seek the truth of the Gospel by listening to it, letting it permeate us, taking time, preparing ourselves. Not after but before entering upon his public life, Jesus chose to spend forty days in the wilderness. Not after but before choosing the companions who were to be his apostles, Jesus spent the entire night in prayer. Yet his relationship with his Father never excused him from preparing for action; it even made further demands on him.

This petition for our daily bread in the Our Father is a

particularly appropriate prayer for the beginning of the day. We acknowledge the good will of the Creator, of the one who tells us:

> And I tell you, Ask, and it will be given you; seek and you will find; knock, and it will be opened to you. For everyone who asks receives, and he who seeks finds, and to him who knocks it will be opened. What father among you, if his son asks for a fish, will instead of a fish give him a serpent; or if he asks for an egg, will give him a scorpion? If you then, who are evil, know how to give good gifts to your children, how much more will the heavenly Father give the Holy Spirit to those who ask him?

We who do not know and do not have, turn to him who does know and does have. We are full of voids that need to be filled, and we turn to him who can satisfy these needs. Amid the horrors and nausea of a world without peace, we are forbidden to keep our suffering to ourselves; rather we must show it to the lifelong, life-giving master.

Jesus asks that we take his remedies as the answers to all our needs. He provides bread for the body, bread for the heart, bread for life. Because it is impossible and totally inappropriate to speak of the kingdom of God to people with empty stomachs, the needs of our own immediate, concrete world are to be inserted at this point in the prayer. We learn to present ourselves with our human poverty before the wealth of God. Then we receive a further surprise: imitating Jesus, with our own lips and a tone of authority, we are to utter the command, "Give us...." I emphasize this point because as God's children, as the children of the household, the Father has decided that he must wait for nothing less than our words, so that he might be able to answer them. Not just any words, of course. Our words here are purified words, spoken with a mature confidence rather than under the yoke of an obligation. These are the words that free us.

In our petitions there are many different choices, from superficial requests to the seeking of true joy. In the early ages of the church, the fathers told us not to remain in an "animal" state in our prayers. By this they meant asking for all our self-interested needs except the very need for God himself. The pursuit of happiness, as the Gospel understands it, is the opposite of how the consumer society understands it. It is so easy to deceive ourselves with too much concern for material gratification. Instead of praying for the riches that endure, we often pursue pipe dreams. For instance, Atlantic City flaunts itself as America's favorite playground, and it attracts millions who go there to bet on their luck. Men I encounter in prison are often the same. They bet their whole life on what they can gain from their crimes. Of course, the odds are against them, just as they are against the vast majority who go to Atlantic City.

Prayer that seeks Life itself, however, takes the form of faithfulness, the clear-sighted attitude of those who know that whatever may befall them, the grace of God will achieve its purposes and God's plan will succeed. We need to know our true hunger, because the food to satisfy it is right at hand. In turn we discover that the food we receive transforms us. We become, as Saint Augustine put it, what we eat. Only Life can give Life. We need the bread of faith. The bread of hope. The bread of endurance.

Even in prison, I find the words of the Our Father about bread resonate less with the ordinary, immediate need for bread for the body (which is always guaranteed by the regulations of the Department of Correction) but more with the desire for the bread that does not perish. This is the only bread that can satisfy a deeper hunger and can liberate the bread that is Jesus himself.

We have that unique, sacred, inexhaustible presence in the mass, the eucharist. That special moment of celebration at Rikers Island is no different at Saint Patrick's Cathedral or Saint Peter's in Rome. It is a moment of awakening and reawakening, of adoration, of communion with the Savior of the world, the Bread of Life. In the mass, we celebrate an action that transcends all times and places. We experience a liberation, a passage in which an entire world shot through with questions and despair can be swallowed up. A prisoner told me: "In my week there are two moments I always look forward to: the Bible class and the mass." Though he was an outsider, in exile, he knew where the true home and the wellsprings were. He would bring his desire and his thirst to them and be transformed by them.

If I had to sum up in a single word my task as a chaplain, I would say it is simply the mass. Everything else before and after—the contact with the prisoners, all kinds of service and friendship—flow from the mass. My task has to do with Jesus coming with his words, his flesh, his blood, into a place that is for him always a chosen place in the midst of sinners—which we all are. Even after thirty-eight years as a priest, I hardly have been able to scratch the surface of what priesthood fully implies. But I do know that it has something to do with what we ask in the Our Father, the Bread of Life.

In my years of formation, the example of witnesses, often priests, was a source of light and direction. I speak of priests just as a soldier finds his models in the army, a physician among physicians, and an athlete among athletes. The companionship of fellow priests who are working at the same task, and the attention I pay them does not mean that I exclude others. Naturally the companionship of fellow workers remains a necessity if I am to develop and make progress. As it says in the Bible: "A brother helped by his brother is a fortified town." Of course, I do not close my eyes to the faults, weaknesses and limitations of these men. But I dare glimpse, and continue to glimpse, something of the great path they follow. Their example serves as a viaticum for whatever span of life remains for me. They had the eucharist in their lives. They had faith. Through it, consistency and meaning shaped their days. I continue to cling to them and hearken back to all those who have passed on, not in order to experience nostalgia for a world that no longer exists, but rather to keep myself from forgetting my inheritance, the immense throng of witnesses. It is a gift from heaven when their unique experience uplifts me, when their individuality speaks to me. All of us draw one another to God. It is a grace to find a warming fire in cold times.

As believers we worship together and there are times in worship when our prayer is wrapped in silence. And this silence is not threatening or oppressive or empty. It points to an activity; it is a silence in motion, a silence in which a man lives and in which he listens for the "still small voice" as Elijah did (1 Kgs 19:12). When we reach the point of being silent together in an unforced way, we have already won a big victory and have attained a real starting point, a stratum of solid rock on which we can build. In a world of noise and turmoil, and often of mockery, we take a major step when we break through the shell of indifference and inattention. A readiness to listen is a precondition for mass everywhere, and all the more so in prison. To begin the mass at Rikers is, first of all, to bring silence. "Silence is two-thirds of devotion," says the Rule of Saint Brendan, according to Dorothy Day. This silence introduces us to the temple of God. And it helps greatly to have some signs of the temple before our eyes. I am thinking here of praying mass in a gymnasium, like it happens in some facilities at Rikers. It is a matter of attitude, inventiveness and respect—all of these are so important. In any setting people hunger and thirst less for bodily needs than for the living word of the Savior, and it is here that the mass comes to their aid. It is the link between death and life in everyday experience; it is a sanctified time.

Every church, whether in or out of prison, should be a sacred space, a place of awe, where we face a majestic God, the Pantocrator of Isaiah 6; the God who passes by in the whirlwind as in Job; the God who seeks the human heart as in Jeremiah; the God of the gentle breeze, whom Elijah knew (1 Kgs 19); the God who is hidden (Is 45:15); and so on. The experience of these surprising, even astonishing encounters with the long-suffering God, at particular moments in our lives, supplies a Christian food, an inexhaustible Christian treasure without which none of us could find our way and make progress.

This awesome encounter with God was made clear to me one morning as a group of teenage prisoners came to mass in the chapel. They had just been transferred from one facility on Rikers Island to the Maximum Security Prison. These young prisoners were being punished for offenses inside the prison; consequently, the Department of Correction was taking special and rather extensive security measures. The group was under close guard when they came to us for the religious service.

This was an event, a precious moment, which a video could have kept magnificently alive. The eyes that looked at us chaplains were the eyes of children who had been wounded for too long and who were exhausted by imprisonment and waiting. Faced with these young people, we had to do everything we could to open a door for them and join them in welcoming Life. Immediately captivated, even fascinated, and fully attuned to us, these "criminals" put off their armor in the chapel. They had no need to grind their teeth or cope with fear. The silence, the light, the colors, everything that helped to identify the place and its objects as sacred, were for them a hitherto unknown or long forgotten pathway. Wisdom and peace advanced toward them and they responded. Their intensity revealed a great deal about the importance of a setting, an environment that influences choices. In this setting prayer could move easily, naturally and authentically. It was not something strange or forced.

The response of these young people also said a great deal about how open we have to be, how sensitive to the depths of a cry that is long buried. As in the age of the cathedrals, when faith was as visible as the very stones, these "young wolves" dried their eyes and rediscovered the word *respect*. Forgotten were the security measures and all the tensions created by surveillance. Even the tour commander said of the occasion: "I find it restful to be here." The living water of faith had its opportunity. It was possible, in this sacred place, for these young men to be fed with real food. Our little community had its thirst quenched and "left" the prison entirely free and full of dignity.

Summary

We need nourishment for both body and soul to walk through our personal deserts each day.

We cannot buy the Bread of Life, as if it were a commercial loaf. We can only ask for the Bread of Life, and must do this one day at a time.

We ask that God give us this day our daily bread. We are a community of people, working each day to make the kingdom come in this world. Ours is a work in progress. Only in the end will the fullness of the kingdom exist.

We bring the things that fill our lives—joys, labors, cares, helplessness—to God each day. We give God "permission," as Mother Teresa often said, to intervene in our lives.

Salvation is not just mere luck. Commitment to the Father's plan is required.

Each morning I have to remember that the reality of the human world has to be connected to another reality that is much more effective: God.

Eucharist, in prison as elsewhere, brings us Life. Our treasure is no less than God.

AND FORGIVE US OUR
TRESPASSES AS WE FORGIVE
THOSE WHO TRESPASS
AGAINST US

You cannot call the God of all kindness your Father if you preserve a cruel and inhuman heart, for in this case you no longer have in you the marks of the heavenly Father's kindness.

De oratione Domini, 3
Saint John Chrysostom

When the team of the space capsule *Endeavor* touched down on American soil on December 13, 1993, it brought back a great hope that was shared by many at NASA and elsewhere. The astronauts hoped they had repaired and given new life to the Hubble Telescope, after it had traveled uselessly through space for years due to a malfunction caused by a manufacturing defect. A colossal failure, an enormous loss of energy, information and money—this was the damage that had to be rectified.

When the experts at the Space Telescope Institute in Baltimore began secret tests to gauge the results of the repair work, what they saw transformed their anxious waiting into explosive joy. The clarity and detail of the pictures sent back to earth turned the telescope into a fantastically successful tool, one even better than they had imagined. "Its eyesight is so sharp," said a scientist, "that if it were sitting in Washington, it could spot a firefly in Tokyo" (*Time,* January 24, 1994). The team and all those involved in the enterprise could be well satisfied. This telescope, the product of their minds and their hands, reached wonderfully into the beyond and thus into the future.

I think of this adventure with its perils, its surprises and its final success, when considering the fifth and most "businesslike" petition of the Our Father: FORGIVE US OUR TRESPASSES AS WE FORGIVE THOSE WHO TRESPASS AGAINST US.

We are born imperfect, with a marked attention for tumbling into the abyss. And yet there is also the unfathomable plan of heaven, with the vision it offers us of being reborn and becoming a child of God. All of us are journeying to God, who is absolute simplicity. We are journeying not because of our own goodness or perfection. On the contrary, when we seek to approach God in his simplicity, we quickly become aware of what is complicated and ugly within us, of what blinds us and defiles us. Sin is part of the unavoidable mystery of the human person, and an understanding of our guilt is necessary. Indeed, it is precious. Before we are able to receive forgiveness, we must have remorse.

How are we to awaken people, to rouse them from the exasperating calm of indifference? It is guilt that stirs up the anthill and changes everything. At Rikers, a prisoner named Rogelio told me, quite seriously; "I am basically a good person," even though his children, all born of different mothers, were scattered. Bill, who had been staying for a week with us at Abraham House in the South Bronx, explained: "I am not a bad fellow. I could have accomplished a great deal here with my abilities." But we, the team managing the house, asked him to leave because he constantly smoked and did nothing else. At a more serious level, there are the stories of revenge, of crimes followed by no remorse, all amid protestations to the contrary. These are everyday occurrences, and not only in Rikers Island.

The consciences of these people have been anesthetized because of misdeeds too often repeated. Their ability to judge themselves soundly has been killed, and they no longer even think they can be forgiven. Thérèse of Lisieux explained that if she had committed all the crimes in the world, she still would turn to the Lord and all her sins would disappear like a drop of water in an ocean of fire. Yes, we can take our guilt to God, for surely we cannot shoulder it alone. As we seek clarity about ourselves and our actions, we first hear the muffled cries for Life—God—in our self-acknowledged failures. Here the human sciences deserve much respect. Yet, the health the psychiatrist seeks and the heavenly health the Gospel gives are not exactly the same thing. Our journey is more like that of a Russian pilgrim in the last century, during which he patiently repeated the same prayer that represented a lengthy process of purification: "Jesus Christ, Son of God, have mercy on me, a sinner."

If we are to make this life journey in the right spirit, we will recognize that while we are on this earth, and usually to the end of our lives, we will have to struggle to embrace the truth. Among the desert fathers of the early centuries, the outcome of their struggle was never in doubt. These men were highly motivated and open to the assistance that heaven never refuses. When I speak of the "fathers," I am referring also to the "mothers," the saints, the tradition and the experience of the church. Faced with all the bitterness, fatalism and exclusiveness that surrounds us, how good it is and how invigorating to rediscover, even in the blackest past or present, a robust optimism, the "Hubble Telescope" of salvation, which, after repairs, points the way and reveals the radiant morning that is our goal.

Human beings do not live on bread alone or on everyday routine. Between the prison made of iron bars and the prisons that our weaknesses create and sometimes justify, the food we need more than any other is the forgiveness of God. Judas's greatest sin was not his betrayal of Christ, but his doubt about Christ's forgiveness. Christ's forgiveness is so passionately offered to us that

Christianity might be summed up in four words: the religion of pardon.

The sin of the world has to be acknowledged, named and destroyed if the world is to breathe. And sin will be wiped away only by forgiveness, a forgiveness that is proclaimed because there has been remorse, a change, a conversion. "...repentance and forgiveness of sins should be preached in his name to all nations, beginning from Jerusalem. You are witnesses of these things" (Lk 24:47–48).

The Our Father sums up everything about forgiveness. Jesus here teaches us a sure way. In a country like the United States, which is so practical and pragmatic, everyone knows the meaning of the word *deal*. The fifth petition of the Our Father is a deal that comes to us from heaven. God's deal is that he is ready to tear up all the bills of our sins on one condition: that we do the same for our debtors. This implies a total obliteration of revenge. Martin Luther King was himself a noble example of this attitude. In return for the healing we give to others, we ourselves find healing. It is when we really acknowledge our own sinfulness that we are able to approach others with words of real liberation. Our own sins are no longer an obstacle.

To illustrate the extent of the revolution that is required, I think of a fine film, *Dead Man Walking*, the story of a man condemned to death and the events leading up to his execution. If it took a Sister Helen to bring the criminal, Matthew Poncelet, into the world of possible forgiveness, think how many will be needed for the alienated families of his victims! Who can explain to these broken people how to rid themselves of their anger? Certainly the best of our poor words are completely inadequate. There can only be silence, a listening from within, eyes fixed on a crucifix, and always a miracle of God: "Father, forgive them, for they know not what they do" (Lk 23:34).

Prison is a place that sows hatred and on Rikers Island hatred is rampant. The prisoners are filled with an intense, suppressed anger ready to explode. "They make me feel like I am less than nothing," one inmate said. And another: "I cannot forgive. I have seen too much." Only moments later another angry man who had experienced only the abuse and corruption of "law and order," hurled these words at me: "Listen to this! My son now talks of becoming a policeman, and I can't stop him!" And then there is the unforgettable image of a man with his wrist in a cast: "I was so damn mad that it was either *hit* the wall or *hit* the captain. Happily, I chose the wall!"

Getting rid of grudges and learning to ask forgiveness for ourselves while granting it to others is another way of experiencing the full force of the radical call given to Jeremiah: "...to destroy...to build and to plant" (Jer 1:10). There is no question here of too easy a compromise, a lack of concern, a flabby passivity. God is always on the hunt for a renewed creation. There is no limitation on his mercy toward those who fear him and seek him.

"What must I do to change? I am fed up with myself! I want to change!" one prisoner pleaded. The same questions are present in the penetrating but silent eyes of the community in the Rikers Island chapel. These men are well experienced with trouble, with wounds. They have no exposure to any other reality. When faced with a world of understanding, one too good to be true, I can see in their eyes the questions that run through their minds: "Is all this true? Can it help me?" Suddenly they pay attention. This is the silent search of so many people in prison. Jesus is the one they are waiting for and they are close to recognizing him. I have witnessed many times those moments when men are ready for something else. Their openness, which can come in the twinkling of an eye, is an immense gift.

If we are to throw off our shackles and our ingrained habits, we need to discover that our real world depends on Someone real, whose name is God, and that this God does away with all the illusions that keep us from seeing that he is our true happiness. We have within us the possibilities of divinization, of which Athanasius, Clement of Alexandria and so many others have sung: "God became a human being so that a human being might teach us how a human being can become godly." That is a whole process that we all must begin and continue, for it concerns not only desperate, fallen, lost human beings, but all of us. God waits on the road for us his children and he so greatly desires to forgive us. He awaits only our willingness to let ourselves be seen. We are, all of us, prodigal sons and daughters.

The first sin as narrated by Genesis consisted of believing too quickly in the tainted claim: "You will be like God" (Gn 3:45). The forgiveness that we gain, although it is always unmerited, frees us from idolatry and restores the youth we lost in Eden by making us "partakers of the divine nature" (2 Pt 1:4). It is nothing less than this "divinization" that my imprisoned friends are vaguely and painfully seeking when they speak of changing. They want to pass from a corrosive association with idols to the new birth that God's forgiveness produces. They want to change masters.

Respect is the first step in such a change. The saints tell

us that we must love Jesus greatly and be willing to understand that our sins not only do us harm but, more seriously and at a deeper level, offend God. Psalm 51 proclaims in truth: "Against thee, thee only, have I sinned...." Our sins cut off the branch that supports us, they extinguish the lamp that illuminates us, and they dry up the spring that quenches our thirst. Our sins hold up love to ridicule.

If we are to realize the full extent of our sin, it will take all the clarity and power of a spiritual telescope. The image of God exists dimly in every human being and our forgiveness of others brings that image to greater light. We have a future. We can be patient. What lies ahead is always better, when we are touched by forgiveness. Now, the present, belongs to something far larger than ourselves. It is as if we have a telescope that measures the universe in a way we never knew before. When the lens is clean, we are forgiven and forgiving, we can see far into the distance. Saint John of the Cross puts it another way: "Purity makes us forget time's long delays." Those are meaningful words for each of us, but especially for those in prison.

Sacramental confessions at Rikers are so different from any human court of justice. Confessions there often resemble those heard in places of pilgrimage: They are spring-cleaning confessions. Confessions become places of rediscovery and also for evangelization. People begin by clearing away the dross, finding a new starting point, and then setting out once more. Years of false starts or vile actions cannot be swept away with a few words when these words are a mere formula. The penitent must understand what he or she has done. Attitude is everything.

Sometimes the confessor must make clear what the

secrecy of confession means. The penitents asks: "This is only between you and me, isn't it?" "No, I tell him, it is between God and the two of us," thereby strongly assuring my partner in this dialogue that I am obliged to secrecy and that I sin seriously if I break that secrecy. I often mention that I go to confession; that the pope and bishops, too, confess their sins, and so on. In short, I try to put the man at ease, for I know only too well that this never easy moment is also a moment of friendship, of the mutual presence of two human beings, and that it is a point of arrival with many old episodes behind it and many new seeds sown.

To go to confession is to set out on a mission. It is to celebrate. "I will sing of thy steadfast love, O Lord, for ever" (Ps 89:1) is also the effect of forgiveness. Ever since the example given by Mary Magdalene, it has been clear that sometimes there had to be very great sins before an immense love could be born. This is often at the heart of turnabouts in our lives; from the stubborn denial of Peter to his blessed acceptance: "But Lord, you know that I love you!"

I often share a French proverb with the prisoners: You start by stealing an egg and you end up by stealing a cow. This is a little illustration that sins are in many cases the result of a lengthy history. Naturally, it will take another lengthy history to get rid of them completely. But all the time required should not frighten them or inflict another wound. The important thing is to be on the right track, even if we are only at the beginning of it. In dealing with a God who does not stop at appearances, everything depends on what is truly essential.

The "right track" is landmarked by our responsibilities, the victims we have created, our repentances, the transformation of remorse into humility, service and much more, and it entails a vast follow-up program. For prisoners as for everyone else, the places from which we start hardly matter. Starting points quickly become a cause for joy when we have learned, with difficulty indeed, what the right goal is. We will finally have perfect vision. God will be accessible to us just as we are. For when we forgive and are forgiven, we touch God.

Summary

God's "Hubble Telescope" points the way to salvation. The Father's deal for us is this: Forgive and you will be forgiven.

We are born imperfect, with a marked attraction for tumbling into the abyss. And yet the unfathomable plan of heaven is that we be reborn and become children of God. To do this, an understanding of our guilt is needed—indeed, is precious. We realize we are journeying to God with the burden of our sins. We have remorse.

Repeated misdeeds anesthetize us; we cannot clearly see our wounds.

God's forgiveness is so passionately offered that Christianity might be summed up in four words: the religion of pardon.

Forgiveness is always a celebration.

AND LEAD US NOT INTO TEMPTATION

God does not want to impose the good, but wants free beings....There is a certain usefulness to temptation. No one but God knows what our soul has received from him, not even we ourselves, and in this way we discover our evil inclinations and are obliged to give thanks for the good that temptation has revealed to us.
De oratione, 29
Origen

On the corner of Ninth Street and Fourth Avenue in Brooklyn stands the imposing church of Saint Thomas Aquinas. The area is commercial, especially as one moves toward Fifth Avenue, with its post office, McDonald's, glut of banks and so on; the sidewalks are often crowded. One sunny morning there was a funeral. Two pallbearers dressed in black were standing near their limousine in front of the church. With nothing to do but wait, their eyes swept the street. The two men in black fixed their gaze on a young couple walking by, arm in arm, lost in their dreams.

Despite its ordinariness, this whole incident struck me deeply. The two contrasting images: the dark glasses of mourning and the rose-colored glasses of the lovers who were alone in the world and focused on their own happiness. I had before my eyes living proof that things around us absorb us and easily imprison us. Who are we to see beyond the immediate to what is distant—eternity? How are we to be fully "in the world without being of the world"? How are we to hear the message of Jesus with its unique words, and not to leave the world? The answer is found in the petition, AND LEAD US NOT INTO TEMPTATION.

As Christians, we need to pray these words of the Our Father with full attention. We often succumb to the deceptive invitation called "temptation" because we are unable to distance ourselves from the immediate and the visible, the realm of instincts and drives. We do not see our limitations; we forget them and make ourselves gods.

Temptation can be anything and everything that interferes or intervenes between us and the source of life. Jesus himself was tempted, beginning with the forty days in the wilderness right through the night of Gethsemane. The difference between him and us is the way in which he struggled, his responses and what they teach. Because he became one of us, he shows us what to say and do at the moment of testing. He is the model of how to control our lusts, our selfish prejudices, our desire to be noticed, our abuses of power.

The first part of the petition is: "Do not lead us." It is something also translated: "Do not let us yield; do not put us to the test." To test, as we know, means to try something to see whether it will hold up, such as when builders test the strength of a cable that will support a bridge. It can also mean to find out whether some claimed competence or expertise is real. This is the reason for army maneuvers and for simulated trial emergencies. Competency comes from practicing. When it comes to God, however, we cannot be tested in these ways, for it would mean that there was something outside God's grasp, something he had still to learn; he would no longer be God. Instead, he waits for us, with a waiting that began at the beginning of the world. He has placed us in this world with the capacity for choice: the choice of becoming free enough to chose him. We have a God who looks for people returning to him from far off, people sufficiently taught by reason and experience to recognize their true home. These people look beyond the surface, beyond the immediate. Because these friends and disciples experience a growing thirst for living water, they also come to know the immensity and depth of God.

Without being able to explain, they know. Without ever having traveled the way, they find it.

It is as if these men and women were all "caught up" like Paul and like Jeremiah, who were seized and thrust into ventures that were in every respect beyond their powers. How long did it take before it dawned on Saint Paul that "for me to live is Christ"? How long did it take him to draw near to "a secret and hidden wisdom of God, which God decreed before the ages for our glorification" (1 Cor 2:7)? How long for the testing that brought enlightenment, for the simple temptation that he outlasted and overcame? If God were to show himself in his true, dazzling reality, no obstacle could resist him, no hindrance would be a match for him. We could not but be drawn, could not but choose him. All alternatives would melt away like snow in the sun or would seem like infantile fantasies. But that is not how it is. On this earth we sometimes hear only silence and find a desert between God and us. Our finite hearts are too small.

The Bible speaks often of how God hides himself and eludes us to some extent. Saint John Chrysostom wrote that "when we are dealing with God, admission of ignorance is the best proof of knowledge." Examples abound that show a distance and an ignorance which we could not overcome were it not for grace: Jacob struggling with the angel (Gn 32), Moses able only to see God's "back" (Ex 34), the divine inscrutability of which the prophets and the psalms speak, and finally, times in the Gospels when "Jesus remained silent." The very fact that God identifies himself with the least of the least (Mt 25) tells us a great deal about the surprising change of attitude required by God. It is as if he were telling us that a sixth sense is needed if we are to learn how to find and recognize him.

We must say yes despite all the limitations of visible reality. We must accept him, not knowing and living helplessly with the vulnerability of a child. When we find bits of evidence in what seems an utterly barren desert, then we truly enter the "re-creative" realm of faith and love. We are able to make a gift even while receiving everything. The impossible becomes possible—all because of "Jesus, the firstborn of a multitude of brothers and sisters" (Rom 8:29).

God, having once chosen to become one of us, cannot will our fall. As Saint James says, "Let no one say when he is tempted, 'I am tempted by God'; for God cannot be tempted with evil and he himself tempts no one" (Jas 1:13). Temptation is often a mirage concealing a chasm. It is an attraction that is followed by an emptiness, sometimes by disgust and, in the best of cases, by remorse. I note "in the best of cases" because if the habit into which we have fallen has dulled even remorse, we are in the area of vice, or what the Bible calls a "hardened heart." Our eyes are blinded and our minds lack landmarks; we no longer know that any light exists.

Because so many of my days are spent in prison, the word *temptation* fascinates me. A prison is often a cemetery for the shipwrecked, the end result of dizzying disasters in which temptation was met and has won the upper hand. How often I have heard men say, "If I had only known beforehand!" From drugs and alcohol, to theft and violence, there is a vast range of deep scars that often seems beyond healing. An entire past may be summed up in the moment of a crime. Physically, mentally and spiritually, a person must go back to the very beginning and renew, reform and rebuild. Everything.

But can a person gain control of his life when everything is fragmented? "I was in court and my younger brother was there. He is twenty-two, I am twenty-four. He told me that my mother had tried to commit suicide and had slashed her wrists. My father is a bastard. When I went to see where he lived, a young woman was there who said she was his wife and had two children by him. I have a brother condemned to life in prison, and now my younger brother is a codefendant with me. I have a sister who sleeps around, I myself may get fifteen years. I would like to take communion because I think it is important." The astonishing thing about this tragic life story of a prisoner encountered by chance is that he told it so easily. But this does not prevent me from seeing in him the pain of an all-encompassing *why* or wondering how to take the first step on the long road ahead. Despite all the obstacles, his willingness to find a way is there.

Faced daily with the excruciating wounds of prison, I turn to the words spoken in Gethsemane; I take them not as a simple piece of advice for others but as a vitally important command for everyone: "Watch and pray that you may not enter into temptation" (Mk 14:38). These words point the way to deal with the reality that must be faced every day. They are saving words. Jesus will never give up on me, but I must still ask his help. And no one needs a diploma or a special competence or advanced knowledge to do that. The Gospel tells us that the little ones, the simple folk and even the ignorant all have the ability to accept and follow the teaching of Jesus. Wherever we find the little ones is the privileged place where Jesus dwells. It is common knowledge in the

Christian experience that the poor become religious more easily than the rich because they are less likely to be self-sufficient, and consequently they are closer to God. And to be poor, according to Jesus, is to be like children. In a true family children are not afraid of their dependence on their mother. It doesn't frustrate them. It is peace, strength and safety. They know where love is. Jesus tells us to imitate them, for they are "the greatest in the kingdom of heaven" (Mt 18:4).

I immediately think of our community in the South Bronx listening to the teaching of Jesus in an ordinary chapel alongside the much larger parish church at Saint Pius on 145th Street. The chapel quickly fills with the men and women from the neighborhood, who gather around the modest cube-shaped altar. There, we experience simple and real moments of faith, accompanied by the strong, clear and very expressive Latin voices from the Caribbean and many parts of South America. Their songs are full of vigor and roll through the chapel like great organ blasts. I do not know whether it is the words, the tone and the melody, or one of these more than the others, that transforms the sacred space. In any case, in that setting, I often think of what I heard a bishop say one day: "The Spanish language is the language of the poor, and it is excellent for paying homage to God."

The people of God had to become the little ones; they had to spend forty years in the wilderness before escaping from their slavery. Despite their nostalgic and envious longing for the "fleshpots of Egypt," for the securities that came with their chains, they emerged from their testing as a people purified and able to enter into a covenant with God. This did not mean an end to their setbacks and struggles. It is, however, one example that shows testing and struggle are among the means used in the divine pedagogy. There is no advance, no substantial progress without it, without purification, humility. This is the good side of temptations, even if it is a costly and perilous side. It is also a basic, constant element for our growth in the human condition. All transitions bring wrenching initiations. None of us reaches maturity without having learned, through our flesh, the lesson that fire burns.

In the midst of inexplicable evil, there are, now and then, moments and gestures of redemption. These moments possess such grandeur and are so sweet-smelling that they silence our cries and force us to completely renew the way we look at things. In the April 1994 issue of *Commonweal,* John Garvey notes:

On March 17 two priests returning from a meeting of the Greek Orthodox Archdiocese were killed as they sat at a stop-light in Queens, New York, waiting for the light to change. Lisa Bongiorno, apparently high on PCP, drove into their car, killing both men instantly. The response was outrage, tabloid headlines with phrases like "priestkiller." Bongiorno, a legal secretary, with a seven-year-old daughter, had no previous record, but said that she had been using drugs for ten years. She has been charged with murder and several other felonies....

George Frangos, Father Demetrios's son, responded to the death of his father in an astonishing way: "The last thing my father would have wanted was to make an example of (Ms. Bongiorno)." ...Frangos has offered to provide a lawyer to help her fight the murder charges....(He) wants Bongiorno to avoid a long sentence, for the sake of her daughter. "We have to look after the innocent one, the child. It is extremely important that her child be told that we forgive her mother."

George Frangos mentioned what his father would have wanted. This story shows not only a man who is extraordinarily capable of forgiveness, but also how good can work almost by a kind of contagion. Saint Seraphim of Sarov said, "Acquire inward peace, and a thousand around you will find their salvation."

If this testing, this accident, had not occurred, we would never have witnessed this forgiveness, this grace. Are we then to put cause and effect in the same balance? Surely not, but it is helpful to remember this incident in our time of testing. How far we are from understanding the mystery of God! This is forgiveness straight from the world to come. "Beloved, do not be surprised at the fiery ordeal which comes upon you to prove you, as though something strange were happening to you. But rejoice in so far as you share Christ's sufferings, that you may also rejoice and be glad when his glory is revealed" (1 Pt 4:12–13).

Summary

Temptation can be anything and everything that could separate us from Life—from God himself....

God has placed us into this world with the capacity for choice: the choice of becoming free enough to prefer him; the choice of taking the entire responsibility for choosing.

Jesus is waiting for us. Jesus cannot allow us to fall, but we must ask his help.

In the midst of inexplicable evil or ordeals, there are, now and then, moments and gestures of redemption. These moments force us to change our ways and how we perceive things.

There is no spiritual progress without struggle, testing, purification and humility. This is the good side of temptations, even if it is a costly and perilous side.

BUT DELIVER US FROM EVIL

The Lord who has taken away your sin and pardoned your faults also protects you and keeps you from the wiles of your adversary the devil, so that the enemy, who is accustomed to leading into sin may not surprise you. One who entrusts himself to God does not dread the devil. If God is for us, who is against us?
De sacramentis, 5,4,30
Saint Ambrose

The Lord's Prayer is truly the summary of the whole Gospel.

De oratione, 1
Tertullian

*I*t is always richly profitable to learn from the history of the church, from what Christians of ancient times did in order to live in Christ. In the long history of the faith experience, with all its dead ends and advances, we see similarities and convergences that cross the boundaries of different societies and cultures. While Vatican II had one eye on the signs of the times, it had its other eye on the past, on the challenges that were met and the answers given, successful or not. The Council did not try to cultivate a nostalgia or rehabilitate what was outmoded or obsolete. It simply tried to keep in mind the gifts, surprises and activities of the Holy Spirit over the course of time. The Council reread the history of God and humanity to renew our awareness of God's presence in our midst.

It is important for our own personal and collective stories of faith in the Bible, but it is equally important to look for them in the postbiblical period as well. We learn this especially from the lives of the saints. Though we are far from having achieved what they did, we can find analogies between their lives and ours. Thus it is never good to turn the saints into strangers by putting them on a pedestal. Why exclude them from humanity? What happened to Christians, for instance, in the remote deserts of Upper Egypt in the third or fourth century A.D. can have meaning in the deserts of our day—even in prison.

Saint Anthony the Hermit lived in the midst of a hellish, daily din and was faced in his temptations with scenes calculated to inspire fear, incite passions and undermine patience. Many painters have tried to capture this on canvas with monsters, snakes, frogs, ghosts and so on. We may choose to regard this anecdote as unimportant and quickly forget it. However, if we dwell on it while reading the life of Saint Anthony, written by another giant of faith, Saint Athanasius, we will understand that the seeming solitude in which Anthony lived was a place of intense and serious activity. In fact, Saint Anthony was engaged in a fierce combat against an adversary of whom the First Letter of John, among others, tells us: "We know that...the whole world is in the power of the evil one" (1 Jn 5:19).

Instead of a blissful place filled with the nearness of God, Saint Anthony's solitude was a combat zone for his hand-to-hand struggle with the forces of destruction. Yet it was an unequal struggle, with Anthony, the friend of God, having the advantage. The adversary whom the Bible calls the devil or demon (Lk 4:2) has only the weight we choose to give him, for the decisive combat has already taken place, and the devil cannot touch what belongs to God. "His power is nothing," said Saint Teresa of Avila, "unless he finds a willingness to submit to him."

Prayer, humility and trust are the weapons near at hand for putting the demon to flight, but too often they become mere words that are distant and irrelevant. Anthony, so far away in time but so close to us in the attacks, disturbances and violence that he experienced, shows us a way. That way is to become the servant of the God who "is" and is completely victorious over "the beast that...was and is not" (Rev 17:8).

I sometimes tell my friends in prison that every morning I must choose between the zoo and Jesus. I call prison a zoo because of the cages, because of the atmosphere, the animal-like existence that often prevails. The massive weight of evil in prison can be read in the eyes; it can be heard in the cries and in the silence; it can be seen behind the scene of commanding officers suddenly responding to an alarm and running with clubs, helmets and bulletproof vests through the corridors. In the face of the merciless brawls, unreal hostility, the stories of frustration, indignities or lies, I wonder whether it is possible to live in such circumstances unless my eyes and heart are resolutely turned to a greater, more inclusive, more profound goal. The exceptional and out-of-the-ordinary are so widespread in prison, that I am made to think a great deal of the exceptional and the out-of-the-ordinary in the life of Saint Anthony. No one working with full awareness in a prison can avoid a radical choice between the zoo and Jesus. The final stage in our journey through the Our Father clearly requires a radical choice, a choice that can rescue us from our many blows and defeats and plunge us into the blessed history of grace.

To confront evil, we do not need to walk in the street with a gun in our pocket. Instead we walk with the Our Father. We keep our eyes on the Master and listen to his sober but sure words that show us the way. "DELIVER US FROM EVIL," placed at the end of the Our Father, makes us realize the struggle is not over, everything has not been settled. This petition compels us to see that we are still on our journey and always grappling with the mystery of iniquity. This "DELIVER US FROM EVIL" is also a prayer to be delivered from all evil that prevents us from growing in love. Evil is a test for us. And the test is a necessary passage. All Christians sooner or later realize that they cannot live a life without pitfalls, that they cannot avoid the desert.

The desert is vast and fearsome, a land of wild beasts and great thirst, but also the birthplace of the covenant with God, the place where God makes water gush from the rock and rains down manna to feed his people. In countless interventions throughout the ages we see that God has willed to show his face to the men and women he has created. We learn, too, that he can greatly manifest himself whenever evil is greatly manifested. Can prison, a place of so much evil, become a place so filled with God?

Far be it from me to glorify prisons or what is abnormal. Too much abnormality over the course of time can even obliterate normal thinking and the perception of harmony and all that is natural. Saint Thomas stated that "A minimum of well-being is needed for the practice of virtue." This minimum is often lacking in our prisons. Faced with this contempt, society cannot ignore Dostoyevsky's warning, "A civilization is judged by what it does with its prisons." These words are appropriately inscribed over the entrance to each New York prison.

The decision to struggle for the betterment of humanity, through word and deed, is simply not a matter of choice. Loving others as ourselves is as much a requirement, Jesus says, as loving God. No one has the right to impose heroism or despair on others. So often our "correctional" systems miss their target and do not rehabilitate but rather worsen the inmates. And we all pay the price as the mass of anger keeps increasing.

In eighteeth century France, during the revolutionary times, priests had to take an oath of hate against the king. Prisons often lead to a similar oath of hate against society. I saw a handicapped man in tears at Rikers when he was left in his wheelchair through the night waiting to be processed and assigned a cell. Another man had his face slashed like a subway map and needed more than two hundred stitches. Still another prisoner had a broom pushed in his rectum by other inmates. I remember Bill, who told me, "Before I kill, I pray." In prison, evil is so excessive, it almost becomes commonplace. How can we overcome this blatant evil? Surely we need to, for when these men leave jail, their anger can do great harm, as we all know but often forget.

Even as I say this, I realize that a society must also be able to defend itself; that it cannot forget the victims or the still vulnerable. There is a need for walls and locks to put criminals out of action and thus prevent them from committing devastating crimes. But when a commanding officer tells me that "to bestow too much care to prisoners, who are insignificant people, is to make monsters of them," he does not even realize how cruel he sounds. After a certain point, human beings begin to sink and get in over their depth. What, in his mind, does "too much care" mean when he is dealing only with "insignificant" people? His illusions about his authority are undermining that authority. He has already lost respect. He is no longer living in a city of human beings, but in a jungle or a warehouse.

In the Bronx, a few days ago, I met three former prisoners who had come out after long terms. I asked each of them what he had learned in prison. One of them, who had spent twenty years "upstate," as prisoners say when speaking of the New York State prisons, told me simply that he had learned nothing. Twenty years with "nothing" is like a tourist facing a sign: "On this site nothing happened." But twenty years with nothing is truly more like a death.

Another of the three men, a sex offender and murderer, after forty-two years behind bars, told me that he had learned to express himself. "You wouldn't have known me; I never opened my mouth and was cut off from everyone. Now I keep nothing back. I have to speak. Yes, that helps me. But what am I to do now? Where am I to go, when I have perhaps twenty-five more years to live?" He was faced with the challenge of starting all over at sixty. A tough situation for a man whose past is always present. What inner resources does he have for carrying such a burden?

I had known the last of the three on Rikers Island. A strong, determined man, he spent fourteen and a half years upstate. He has something in him of Jean Valjean, the courageous, unbeatable hero of *Les Miserables*. Before his release in 1995, I had been to visit him in Dannemora, in Green Haven. "I believe that I spent the entire time with respect and dignity. I read, I learned, I changed, I wanted a positive result: to be able, by my attitude, to give something back to the society." I was overjoyed to see him. Here before me was a mature man, enriched by having passed through the fire, open to what is ahead and even to the rejections he will inevitably meet. "I hide nothing in my resumé." He said, "I keep to the truth. Now I only have to learn again how to take the initiative in my life. In prison they always told me what I had to do. It will turn out all right." Despite his wonderful attitude, I could see him looking thoughtful and a bit vulnerable as he turned from me with the words: "This is the first time I'll be taking the subway by myself, at night. I'll have to be careful."

It is said that the steps by which a person becomes an addict manifest themselves in chronological order. Those steps are reversed when that person tries to break out of his addiction. In other words, when a person begins to depend on alcohol or drugs, he first loses his self-esteem and his sense of spiritual value understood in the broadest sense. He loses the sense that his life has meaning. The process begins with what is deepest and most sacred to us.

The next level affected is the mental. Due to the effects of alcohol, of drugs, thinking becomes disturbed and confused; the mind loses its benchmarks and accepts the illogical and the unbelievable. A man told me: "If I had now to choose between a bottle and a thousand dollars, I would take the bottle." He was no longer using the language of reason. Finally, the physical level is affected: the loss of health, the decay of the organs. This opens the door to both pain and physician, while waiting for the worst.

When the time comes to halt this descent into the hell of addiction, the way back follows a reverse chronological direction. The ascent is begun at the physical level, then the mental level is addressed before reaching the spiritual, which is essential to functioning fully as a human being. These different levels or stages do, of course, overlap, but it is only the last, the spiritual, that marks a completion, a wholeness recovered or in the process of recovery. There may be temporary setbacks, but as the addiction begins to be controlled, success is again possible. Like the team of astronauts on the Apollo 13 space flight who, having brought the crippled craft back to earth safely, proclaimed their mission "a successful failure," a person emerging from addiction is another example of a successful failure. These words are a perfect description of

111

the liberation from evil that can take place in prison or elsewhere. It is a victory in spite of weakness.

The possibility of rebirth exists whatever our history or situation. Here again there are levels or stages, but the progression surely takes place. We start with our mistakes, even our catastrophes. When these are given to God in repentance, they bring salvation. Everything depends on knowing that there is someone to whom we can give our sins, and that he not only exists but is waiting for us. "DELIVER US FROM EVIL" brings us to safety; we have achieved our goal. A Swiss Cardinal, Charles Journet, used to say in his retreats that this last petition, "Deliver us from evil," is the summation of the entire Our Father. When there is no more evil, the kingdom of God comes, the Father's name is hallowed, his will is done and so on. The liberator can transform everything.

It is only human that we think of ourselves first and rely on ourselves, even in our prayers. But with the Our Father as a treasure, we turn totally to God. Indeed we learn to swim in that unfathomable ocean too deep for words, the immense reality of God. I think that we die or live depending on what we do or do not do with this prayer, the Our Father, which Jesus came to give us along with his life. Whoever you are, and no matter what kind of prison or desert you are in, remember: This very day you can be set free.

As an example of the transformation of a life in God due to prayer and faith, I would like to share with you the last letter written by a prisoner a few hours before being guillotined in 1957. His name is Jacques Fesh. He had killed a policeman in Paris during a bank robbery and was condemned to death. The course he followed to enter into Life offers us an extremely powerful witness, one bathed in the power of God, filled with welcome, acceptance and a high forgetfulness of self. Starting from the dead-end ways of a second-rate youth, he finally met Love in prison. It seems to me that this letter, the final expression of a human being an inch away from death (and yet how alive!) opens heavens to us. Jacques Fesh, a child whom God loved to the point of folly, became incredibly free within himself. May I admit here that I pray to him every morning? His prison has vanished. There is now only joy, "exceeding joy" (Ps 43:4).

September 30, 1957
Dear Mother,

We have written to each other so much in the last six months that in this final letter I can only urge you to persevere on your path. You have already made some progress because you know the means to be used. Try to open your eyes wide and see behind this apparent punishment a manifestation of God's will, which is Love. Do not clutch your pain too much, give it to God and suffer for one reason alone: the sins committed against God. My death, you see, is the great goal of life. We are all mortal and sooner or later we will all leave this valley of tears; the important thing is to leave it in good condition.

As for me, be assured that God has given me the great grace of drawing me to himself, and when you read these pages, I will be seeing our Lord Jesus Christ. I admit that I am somewhat afraid of your hasty reactions under the pressure of deep sorrow. Above all, stay calm, do everything with moderation, and try to let your distress melt away in the love of Jesus, who waits only for your call so that he can come and console you. Leave all justice, all vengeance in the hands of God; that is my formal wish. Christ came to save the world, not to condemn it. Let us not condemn ourselves, even if others do.

Seek peace; if you are willing, you have an important and beautiful part to play. Much depends on you, much will be asked of you, but as a result much will also be given to you on the condition that you do not resist. I wish with all my heart that in time you may be reconciled with our holy Mother the Church. She distributes all the gifts of Christ, and in rejecting her you deprive yourselves of all the remedies, benefits, and graces that Christ has entrusted to her. Reflect carefully on this.

Dear Mother, first of all I thank you very much for all the love you have shown me during these last months. I have in front of me the pile of letters you sent me and which have strengthened me. I have made them the center of my days, and without them I would have suffered much more. You know what Jesus says in his Gospel: "I was in prison and you visited me." When you wrapped your child in your love, you also touched Christ and I am quite sure he will reward you for it. Do not forget that charity covers a multitude of sins! If much seems dry or incomprehensible, you can rise above it through charity. Charity is gentle and patient; it believes everything, hopes for everything, and will never end. Do not forget that God is Love!

I hereby entrust to you my little daughter. Protect her lovingly, without spoiling her. Bear in mind that Jesus loves her infinitely, and what you do to one of these little ones, you will be doing to him. Love her in God and be sure that up there I will be protecting and watching over her with all the love of Jesus; that love will fill my mind. As for yourself, remain in the love of Christ and you will see God.

Well then, my life is over. My head will fall "like a little spring flower which the owner of the garden plucks for his own pleasure" [Saint Thérèse of Lisieux]. A gloriously shameful ending, with heaven as its reward! I am happy.

Good-bye, dear Mother, and may the Lord protect you and all those you love. I embrace you in Christ and Mary.

Your son in God,
Jacques

Summary

To confront evil, we do not have to walk around with a gun in our pocket. We walk with the Our Father.

The adversary that the Bible calls the devil or demon only has the weight we choose to give him. The weapon to put him to flight is close at hand.

The petition, "DELIVER US FROM EVIL" helps us realize the struggle is never over during our lifetime on earth, everything has not been settled. We are still on the journey and grappling with the mystery of iniquity.

The words *successful failure* are a perfect description of the liberation from evil that can take place in prison and elsewhere.

Jesus came to earth to give us his life and, let us never forget, to teach us the Our Father. These are treasures that are accessible everyday of our lives.

---●●●---

ABRAHAM HOUSE

In the Name of Our Father Who Art in Heaven

When painting the faces on icons, the artists use a method called "progressive clarification." Before achieving the radiant image they first apply many shades of somber dark colors. On top of these colors they add progressively lighter tones of yellow until the face becomes aglow. The work of these artists is truly a spiritual experience. It is the work of moving from darkness to light. An icon is, above all, a glimmer of heaven.

Just as with the progressive clarification in icons, some prisoners are able to move from the dehumanizing experience of having to relate to Our Father in hell to the dignity of addressing God in heaven. Abraham House comes about to join these prisoners on their journey.

The Need for Abraham House

Every day there are headlines and debates about crimes and criminals. The media and politicians have something to say about prisoners, about juvenile violence, about waging a war on crime, about the construction of more prison cells.

Abraham House, located on Willis Avenue in the South Bronx, also has something to say about prisoners and all those other subjects, but it is something hopeful. Nationally, about three out of four inmates, when released from prison, return to crime—and ultimately to jail—but Abraham House, through its small community program to prepare inmates for release, has shown that these appalling national statistics can be reversed.

Mott Haven, the neighborhood in which Abraham House is located, is the poorest congressional district in the United States. Nearly everyone living here has been in jail or knows someone doing time. When Jonathan Kozol wrote his 1996 best-seller, *Amazing Grace,* about Mott Haven, he quoted a fifteen-year-old neighborhood girl who, even at that tender age, knew enough about jail to use it as an analogy to explain her existence in this poor community: "It is not like being in jail exactly. It's more like being hidden. It's as if you have been put in a garage where, if they don't have room for something but aren't sure if they should throw it out, they put it there where they don't need to think of it again." Why does Abraham House exist in this community where the poor are ware-housed by society? Quite simply, here we have been welcomed; in half a dozen other communities where we sought to put down roots, neighbors were adamant: "Not in my backyard!"

Abraham House grew out of the frustration of some Rikers Island chaplains and correction officers who watched men and women inmates, seemingly eager to change their lives, fail utterly upon their release. Why these failures despite the best intentions?

The shock of being free can be greater than the shock of being incarcerated. Ex-offenders return to their neighborhoods and families with big needs. They can quickly become frustrated and angry, living with a stigma that often prevents them from getting jobs and leading normal lives. I remember a man, just twenty-seven, telling me he had been jailed thirty-two times. As a chaplain, stories like this oblige me to turn away from resignation and passivity. Out of this, ultimately, came Abraham House, which is unique.

Our ministry draws directly on the words of Jesus: "I was in prison and you came to visit me." Jesus told us that he is to be found in prison. So our work reaches between the world inside and the world outside. Our goal, from the start, was to minister to the spiritual, mental and physical needs of offenders to insure a different kind of reentry experience on their return to life outside. We wanted to set up a "house of prayer" for prisoners, their children, their families and for those visibly or invisibly present. Prayer inside Rikers would naturally be joined to prayer on the outside of the prison.

A prisoner named Fred explained the need for such a parish far better than I could. He wrote these words in a Rikers cell block:

To have a place on the outside for us to worship has been needed since the opening of Rikers Island over sixty years ago. For me, and for many I have talked with, there has always been something missing, some added measure of assurance. When we first learned that Abraham House might be this sort of parish, you could see it on our faces and feel the energy of our hope.

Many inside and outside these bars want to help, to change things around. But no one seems to know how. I believe that this church will not only be the first real, meaningful step for us here, but it will be the single most important step in changing the religious, social and crime status in all New York City.

A lot of people—clergy, judges, communities and political leaders—are up day and night working on complex solutions to our city's problems involving crimes and criminals. There are job-incentive tax breaks to employers who hire ex-cons. There have been drug programs and this, that and the other thing. The problem is when we inmates come home and there is no place to go.

We soon believe that all the stuff we have heard and loved about Christ is just a gimmick to sell shoes. If, in spite of this, we still search, we discover that we cannot find Christ alone; we need fellowship, a community of Christ-searchers. But we often can't get in (some churches shun us). So we go where we are welcome with a hug and a smile; with a joint of weed, a bag of dope and a gun. Back to the street and a life of no holds barred.

With all the violence and crime in this city, what puzzles me is why a church hasn't already been set up for us. It is time we made the move that will make the difference.

Abraham House's very purpose has been to meet Fred's challenge. Abraham House seeks to build relations. Fred understood that it is impossible to be an individual Christian. Faith in God, our Father, means deep union with sisters and brothers, the community, the multitude. Prayer at Abraham House has to be a we-prayer.

The Struggle to Begin Abraham House

We began with a fledgling program in Brooklyn in 1991 and opened Abraham House in Mott Haven in 1993. Our program only took root after many withering attempts and dead ends. "We'll be in touch; give us your phone number." "I don't think you will get this empty convent. Six months ago the pastor refused to rent it to handicapped boys." "The government is interested in material things. It doesn't know how to evaluate compassion and counseling. That does not appear in the bureaucrat's book." "Avoid spiritual things. Focus on organization, work-release programs." "We cannot offer you this place. You will get it only if the State of New York gives you the money." "You are welcome to live in this rectory, but no group of people will be allowed to come here. You will be able to meet people only individually and in this office near the front door." "People in the neighborhood do not at all like the idea of a house for criminals."

On an April day in 1993 Catholic Charities called, offering a Mott Haven building at 342 Willis Avenue. Its name was "Fifteenth Station, Inc./My Family Place," a shelter for ten or so men who, after the administration had pulled out of the program, had become squatters and trashed the building. All we had to do was to tell Catholic Charities that we were interested. It would take five months to make the place livable, but we rejoiced at having a starting point. On Easter Sunday, April 11, three Little Sisters of the Gospel and myself signed leases for apartments close by our forlorn building. Several priest friends told us: "You'll see; one day there will be a resurrection." We will remember Easter, 1993.

The start-up money for the renovation came from Belgium, the native country of Sister Simone Ponnet, who would become Abraham House's executive director and who, for nineteen years, has been chaplain at Rikers Island. In 1992, Sister Simone was invited to speak on Belgian television about her ministry with prisoners. Many people were moved and provided financial help.

From France, too, we found benefactors. This money was a godsend, financing the renovations that Tito, a contractor friend, undertook. Of course, the money didn't last long, but other Belgians vacationed with us, and spent time cleaning, painting and helping in whatever way was needed. By September we had beds for twelve residents, a clean yard and a magnificent chapel.

We decided to call this place Abraham House for many reasons. Abraham is the father of believers. He was a man on a journey throwing himself fully into his calling. He knew how to trust. He was an old man, with a whole life behind him, and yet a man of the future. He obeyed completely because he believed. Abraham was a man of hospitality, of prayer, of intercession, who said to God many times: "If there are people in the city who are just, you would spare the city, wouldn't you?" And then there is the beginning of chapter 15 in Genesis: "Don't be afraid, Abram; I am your *shield.*" Since at Rikers the word shield means the badge that allows a person to go freely through all doors, it seems only appropriate to recall this Old Testament line: "Don't be afraid, Abram; I am your shield." The last, but not the least reason for calling this place Abraham House was the fact that the biblical patriarch is held in honor by Jews, Moslems and Christians, all of whom are welcome here. In our troubled and divided world, Abraham speaks to us of unity and peace.

We finally dedicated Abraham House on September 29, 1993. Our chapel was too small for the seventy or eighty people who came. Joining Manhattan Auxiliary Bishop Patrick V. Ahern were our friends, those who know that this house exists because Rikers exists.

We have found a lot of "soul food" in witnessing the healing that is possible among inmates and their families when prayer is given priority. We base our work, our commission, on faith in all that God has told us. Prayer plays a large role in our work, just as it did when Moses confronted Amalek, Israel's enemy: "Whenever Moses held up his hand [in prayer], Israel prevailed" (Ex 17:11). In chapter nine of Saint Mark's Gospel a sick child is brought to Jesus after his disciples are unable to heal the youngster. Jesus cures him and explains: "This type of sickness can be cured only by prayer." Jesus gives us this key. He wants us to practice and experience the meaning, the promise of his words, which is a vital part of the Abraham House program of rehabilitation.

It has been said that the decision to pray is the most critical one an individual makes in his or her spiritual life. A poster hangs at the door of Abraham House listing the names of men and women from all parts of the globe who pray for Abraham House around the clock. Whatever their religion, each has committed himself or herself to praying for Abraham House thirty minutes a week at a specific time. These people are part of our hidden, effective community. They provide a real boost, a gift, our best insurance policy. We treasure the part they play in Abraham House as it seeks to heal, to provide full recovery, full living, to former prisoners.

The Program at Abraham House

If our program were to have any unity, of course, it had to be well organized. We see this need and continue to see it. In our Residential Program the participants are placed in our custody by judges. They are taught to examine their lives and past mistakes and understand why they are in their present situation. Through group and personal counseling, they learn to accept responsibility and acquire the social skills needed to return successfully to society. Their activities and progress are monitored, they learn job disciplines and are challenged to believe more deeply in God and in themselves. They need to achieve wholeness to build their new lives. If there were sufficient funding for additional staff, we could fill the house. there are certainly more than enough potential residents.

Nonresident Services. Abraham House provides supervision and guidance to other prisoners who are placed in its custody but permitted by the courts to reside with their families. Generally minors and women with children, these people receive the same intensive individual instruction and rigorous direction as our residents. In addition, the Bronx District Attorney assigns inmates to Abraham House who have been sentenced to community service. These individuals are specially selected because they require additional counseling and one-on-one assistance.

Abraham House also provides the service we call The Good News Family Center. A stigma is attached to having a family member in prison; often these people are shunned. The problems of prisoners' families often multiply when, because of language difficulties, they are unaware of the public services available and their legal rights. The Center, which attracts many immigrants from Central and South America, offers personal sessions with volunteer attorneys, not to prepare cases but simply to take the baffled and frustrated through the bureaucratic maze. Private counseling across a wide spectrum is offered by professionals, and classes in English as a second language and computers are also available. Good, wearable clothes are supplied to those in need, many of whom are single mothers. Sister Amy Henry, a chaplain and Little Sister of the Gospel, spends a lot of her time visiting families of prisoners. Always on the road and ready for the extra mile, she has a tremendous gift for finding people and making connections with them.

Abraham House also operates a Food Pantry Program under the supervision of Sister Rita Claus, a nurse in a detox center in Manhattan. She is helped by our residents. We serve about fifty Mott Haven families and another thirty-five families of prisoners. Each receives weekly canned foods, dry milk, cereals, rice and snacks. Our most recent outreach is the Good News Youth Center, thanks to the tremendous help of the Marist Brothers. They have become a vital part of Abraham House. Marist Brother Michael Flanigan is now our full-time youth director. We have no words for the passion, openness and friendship we found in this group of brothers. An alternative to the streets, the Center provides a safe, secure and welcoming place where the young can come to socialize, relax or receive social services such as after-school tutoring and individual counseling. A local gym is available twice a week for basketball and weight training. Our focus: to enable young people to see their value as individuals and encourage them to be active participants in their neighborhood. Group meetings are held on topics such as parenting, teenage pregnancy, nonviolence as an alternative, conflict resolution and social skills training (i.e., how to conduct oneself at job interviews with adults). The Youth Center also counsels and directs the day-to-day activities of more than a dozen youths who have been in trouble with the law and have been assigned to us by the courts.

As things are, we operate at about 75 percent capacity.

We are confident that this house has all the elements that it needs to be effective. Surely it has proven itself. Not one of the inmates who have graduated from Abraham House's residential program has resorted to crime; instead, they are holding jobs and getting on with their lives.

The Vision of Abraham House

The core and foundation of Abraham House is based upon the belief that Jesus Christ is the head of the house and that the way of the Gospel is the underlying foundation of our existence. That's why we have religious services in a chapel. A Pastoral Center is open to all on Saturdays and Sundays. We already saw that Abraham House draws its name and inspiration from this forefather of all Christians, Jews and Muslims. This makes Abraham House a nonsectarian program of the Catholic Archdiocese of New York. Whatever their faith, men and women who are in our program are called upon to believe, as Abraham did, more deeply in God and in themselves.

One of the unique elements in the Abraham House approach is a close involvement with the families of the men who will be participants in our program. Through family support and counseling during their stay, as well as after completion of the program, we want to ensure their fruitful reentry into society.

The second important dimension in the Abraham House program is to provide a place where the emotional, moral and social needs of ex-offenders are addressed. These men must learn that personal growth is ultimately their responsibility; positive behavior is to be affirmed at Abraham House and negative behavior must be accounted for; learning to live in community is essential.

We are proud of some results. We do not pretend to have all the answers. Our dream is a place of hope. Those who want to change can find here the possibilities to do it, because the entire atmosphere of this house is one of hope. "Each Saturday at Abraham House, I find Life," said one mother. Because of their accumulation of problems and their despair in finding a solution, these very vulnerable people find a refuge at Abraham House. Here, every weekend, we have a very clear reflection of the consequences of prison, and we also have a place of hope.

In short, our vision is that Abraham House never tire of the mystery, the pain, the privilege of being human. That Abraham House never forget the reconciling, liberating, transforming mystery of God. From anger to worship. God's love has no end.

The Helping Hands of Abraham House

Right from the beginning of our efforts we had such tremendous support from a whole network of people, starting with Jacques Travers, a magnificent brother, "the saint of Brooklyn," since deceased. When we needed courage the most it was Jacques who gave us his generous unconditional support. He often came to Rikers—a very short man with a tremendously huge heart, so resolute in his actions and in his work for the faith. He said one day: "Yes, I have eliminated authoritarianism, violence and lying from my conduct absolutely, because that style is neither Christian, nor human, nor effective." His house was a home for so many little people. Said he so many times: "Let's help one another. Let's not be too late to love." This man is really in the foundations of Abraham House.

We found helping hands among the very people we

met in Rikers every day. I mean the correction officers at all levels of authority. We saw and we learned that it is not easy to run a jail. We saw people of good will dreaming with us about Abraham House. I would like just to quote one of them, William Sutton, who served at Rikers Island for more than twenty-one years and now is on the board of Abraham House:

> I watched prisoners return, over and over, and actually saw these men grow old in jail. I labeled it the revolving door syndrome. I was the officer in charge of work details, and it was my responsibility to interview and assign inmates to jobs. Because of this, I had access to personal information about these men. The record showed most returned to jail because of a "lack of direction." Many only needed a little support in changing their lifestyles, but those programs, which could be so productive, do not exist in prison. It was normal that I wanted to reach out to prisoners who needed help to lead a different life. Father Peter and Sister Simone approached correction and community-oriented people to develop a sound program. Abraham House has not changed its goal and purpose. We have remained steadfast in holding to our true vision, which can be summed up in the Chinese proverb; "Give a man a fish, and you feed him for one meal. Teach a man to fish, and you feed him for a lifetime."

Our first Compassion and Justice award has been presented to the Honorable Leslie Crocker Snyder, Supreme Court Judge of New York and to Father Benedict

Groeschel. These impressive backers have given a tremendous boost to Abraham House.

Financially Abraham House runs on a shoestring. It relies on nontraditional and cost-effective approaches. Although we had provided funds from George Soros's Open Society Foundation, a supporter of innovative approaches in the criminal justice field, and from other people, this part of our life is a permanent concern. Here it is good to remember what John Cardinal O'Connor, Archbishop of New York, said to us on one of his visits to Abraham House: "My responsibility is to try to open many, many Abraham Houses. You have my word: I will try to help bring that about. I will try to help get the money. I will try to help deal with the authorities. This is one of the most impressive activities I have seen in New York, one of the most impressive in which the church is involved. Lives are not simply rehabilitated, but saved here. Families are being restored. Consider the productive work that will be done by those who have gone through Abraham House, and the savings to society."

OUR FATHER...Continues at Abraham House

Abraham House is not yet reaping a rich harvest. Even if we help only one person on the journey from the old, hardened anger to the new world of adoration, our work is successful. In the light of the Gospel the measurement of successes and failures is never the same as that of the society. Little things are never little. The three dozen men and women, former prisoners, who have taken part in our residential program are making success of their lives. Meanwhile, our parish is flourishing with more than four hundred families in our network. This includes families of cons and ex-cons, ex-inmates, spouses, girlfriends, children and so forth. Our communication is not just formal or anonymous. Prison life isolates. Our approach is the opposite. We hope the small size of Abraham House and its parish and Pastoral Center will always make a more intimate, familiar approach possible.

We know we are on a journey. We begin not knowing him—or how to pronounce his name. But as we move ahead, we begin to imagine and understand, and ultimately to experience a blessed, powerful, gracious intimacy with Our Father that we never expected.

At last we learn who we are, no longer strangers but

ONE FAMILY, ONE PEOPLE WITH OUR FATHER.

OUR REAL FATHER/MOTHER IN HEAVEN

Creator of the Infinite, the Simple,
   Intimate of the Ineffable,
   Worker of Wonders,
Before all, After all, Everywhere.
   Music, Silence
Rock, Ocean, Breath, Fire.
   Let our eyes drink in your Beauty.
   Sole preserver of the universe,
   Let our every moment breathe in
   The always greater Eternal One who is
            YOU
In our thirst, in our hunger never let us forget the
            WAY
To your freely given, delectable
            TABLE.

      Teach us to hate hatred,
the murderous look, the cancer of the heart.
Do not let the ugly abyss of ugly desire
        Swallow us up.
Break our chains. Crush the evil in us.
        Amen.